The Space Shuttle Program fired the imagination of a generation. A ship like no other with its place in history secure, Scott's first-hand accounts and unique art continue the mission to inspire the next generation of possibilities. C. F. Martin Sr., our founding father, would be proud of that legacy. So it is fitting to have one of Scott's art pieces exhibited alongside the first American guitar in space, in the C. F. Martin Museum that celebrates Martin's vital place in America's ever-evolving musical culture.

Dick Boak
Director of Museum, Archives & Special Projects
C. F. Martin & Co., Nazareth, Pennsylvania

Scott hit the universal sweet spot with his shuttle art and first-hand accounts of the American Space Shuttle adventure. The reader will readily relate to this beautifully written book by recalling when and where they were during these historic events. I commend Scott for dedicating his entire career to the success of the External Tank. He indeed made a BIG difference for the Space Shuttle Program.

Jim Kennedy
Former Director
John F. Kennedy Space Center

REMOVE
BEFORE FLIGHT

Jacoby,
Reach for the
STARS !

Scott "Shuttleman" Phil.

" 2017 "

This is a story you haven't heard before, a "must read" for any space aficionado

Michael D. Griffin
NASA Administrator, 2005-2009

REMOVE
BEFORE FLIGHT

Scott "Shuttleman" Phillips
Memoir of a Space Shuttle Team Member
with Dianne Phillips

TATE PUBLISHING
AND ENTERPRISES, LLC

Published by Tate Publishing & Enterprises, LLC
127 E. Trade Center Terrace | Mustang, Oklahoma 73064 USA
1.888.361.9473 | www.tatepublishing.com

Tate Publishing is committed to excellence in the publishing industry. The company reflects the philosophy established by the founders, based on Psalm 68:11,
"The Lord gave the word and great was the company of those who published it."

Book design copyright © 2014 by Tate Publishing, LLC. All rights reserved.
Cover Design by Gary Milgrom with Jim Villaflores
Interior design by Mary Jean Archival

Published in the United States of America

ISBN: 978-1-63367-500-1
Biography & Autobiography / Personal Memoirs
14.10.10

To all of my Shuttle team members for
recognizing and sharing in my vision

To my soul mate and loving wife, Dianne,
for giving voice to my story

To Christian and Tyler for your
enthusiasm and support

To my father, Dick Phillips,
1932–2004

And my brother, Steve Phillips,
1956–2013

Space Shuttle Logo

Contents

Foreword

S cott Phillips' book, *Remove Before Flight,* is one that offers a different view of the Space Shuttle Program than anything you are likely to have read by anyone else involved in America's space program. This is not a memoir by an astronaut, a flight controller, or a senior engineer or manager. Instead, it is a view of the program as seen by one of "the guys on the ground," someone who spent thirty years inside the program, helping to carry out the day-to-day work to assemble, prepare, and launch the incredibly complex and sophisticated machine that we knew as the Space Shuttle.

Seen from afar, the Shuttle was so beautiful and flew so gracefully that onlookers could easily forget that it was a six-million-pound brute of a machine, a mass of industrial equipment requiring thousands of people to service and launch. Those who managed this over the three decades of the Shuttle Program were the greatest work force in American history, maintaining heavy, sometimes dangerous equipment, toxic propellants, and incredibly fragile instruments and systems, often from precarious positions or in confined spaces. And they had to do it exactly right, for human life was at stake, both on the ground and in space, in the most public manner possible.

Scott Phillips was one of those people, and this is his story. It is told movingly and well, with the humility that comes from knowing that he was just one of many thousands involved in the launch of each Space Shuttle, but also with the pride that comes from knowing that he was, in fact, one of those thousands.

Michael D. Griffin
NASA Administrator, 2005–09

5,4,3,2,1...and we have liftoff!

Prologue

Mudman

I was working as a mechanical technician performing critical pre-flight testing on the Space Shuttle's external liquid oxygen tank designed to hold over 143,000 gallons of fuel at launch. Months earlier, our team had installed stamp-sized measuring instrumentation called strain gauges. On this day in September 1979, our task was to conduct stress analysis on the tank to verify that the weld seams would hold the fuel during the Shuttle's fiery ascent. NASA decided to use barium sulfate—driller's mud—to simulate the 1.3 million pounds of liquid oxygen.

After verifying the integrity of the tank, we had to drain the mud and clean the residue off the walls. To do this, the Bendix Corp. had created a 36-inch-diameter platform, called a Man Tube, which rotated 360 degrees on a thin cable system to lower a person, in a standing position, through the top of the liquid oxygen manhole with a high-pressure water hose to spray the walls. The Man Tube was hooked at the top by a winch cable that was manually lowered incrementally as the walls were cleaned.

Because it was in a confined space, this undertaking was extremely dangerous and required tank-entry certification.

The Man Tube had never been previously tested with an actual person. This was our first attempt, and because I was the youngest, at twenty years old, thinnest, and looking back, perhaps the most naïve member of the team, I was selected to be the guinea pig. We were working the night shift, so the on-site safety personnel were slim, but we naturally assumed the tube would work as designed. I donned the waterproof white-hooded suit, which included a built-in breathing apparatus that provided enough oxygen for my five-hour mission, and a pair of rubber gloves. I felt like an astronaut anticipating his first mission, and I was excited to perform my first solo task.

Scott in the Man Tube. Courtesy NASA

As I looked down between my feet through the metal grate into the tank, it was daunting knowing there was only one way in and one way out. I quickly tried to purge myself of any thought of claustrophobia or fear of falling into the cave-like tank. As my team members cranked me down the dark abyss, I had the eerie feeling of being in a casket. I was dropped ten feet at a time as I dangled in the Man Tube by one thin cable and flood lamps overhead created tremendous heat.

Looking down through the grate of Man Tube. Courtesy NASA

The darkness finally eased as the floodlights filtered through the manhole, illuminating the tank. The combination of heat and blinding glare reflecting off the shiny aluminum tank walls—the portion that had not been covered with mud—caused me to become disoriented. I didn't know which way was up or down. The pulsating hose was activated, and I began to blast the tank walls. The intense pressure caused the tank to reverberate, dramatically increasing the noise level. Without hearing protection, my fatigue accelerated and communication with my team was compromised. As I completed my first dizzying 360-degree rotation, mud splattered onto my face shield, and I was soon completely covered in the heavy sludge.

About 45 minutes into the process, at 40 feet down, the air hose popped off of my suit. This horrifying revelation was confirmed when I heard the spring clip hit the bottom of the tank with a loud clink. By then, I was already overheated and exhausted from the noise and struggling with the force from the hose. I was fighting a nauseating, spinning sensation. When I lost air pressure, my face shield instantly fogged over, distorting my vision. I desperately gasped for air. Instinctively, I grabbed my walkie-talkie. "Get me the hell out now!" I screamed. "I've lost my air supply! We need to abort!"

The agonizingly slow process began as my team had to hand crank the winch to bring me back up. I had lost track of how far down I was, and I tried to determine how far I had to go. As I cleared a small patch on the interior of my shield with my tongue, I looked up at the narrow passage above. I was alarmed that the manhole cover appeared to be about the size of a dime.

With a limited oxygen supply, I intuitively knew to maintain shallow breathing. I had to leave my hood on, but thankfully, my certification training had taught me not to panic in a confined environment. I tried to keep my thoughts positive and focused, and I slowly reviewed the details of the operation. I ascertained that the mud had lubricated the spring clip on the air hose, causing it to pop off. When I finally emerged, I was covered from head to toe in mud. I was reeling and lightheaded but elated to draw in the fresh air. It took at least fifteen minutes to raise me out of the manhole—the longest fifteen minutes I've ever experienced before or since.

A NASA photographer was on-site to document the procedure of me going down into the tank. But by the time I was back on top, everything including lights and equipment was also completely encrusted in the mud, and he had gone. It is not customary for NASA to release pictures of this nature, but they provided a few photos to our quality and safety people. I was inspired to document the incident myself and hijacked a couple of the pictures. No one ever knew I had them—until now.

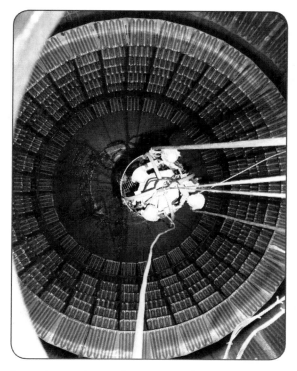

Scott being lowered into the interior of tank. Courtesy NASA

The quality and safety team members who were present on the night shift chose not to write an incident report. We performed our own modifications to the suit and rewrote the procedures. We passed the information on to the next day's shift, and they successfully completed the work. Although the weight-testing itself was successful, the mud had corroded the tank after the residue dried. Many man-hours were spent using stainless-steel brushes to remove the corrosion. Fortunately, this tank was used only for testing and was not intended for a flight.

Liquid Oxygen tank dome corrosion after
removal of mud. Courtesy NASA

This was the first close call of my career, but not the last. It made me realize how hazardous our work was and reinforced the importance of always being vigilant.

By the way, for performing this risky mission, I received an extra 50-cent-an-hour night-time differential!

Humble Beginnings

On July 20, 1969, I gazed into the star-studded night sky and tried to grasp what I had witnessed hours before. That day, Neil Armstrong became the first man on the moon. I was barely ten years old and living less than 100 miles from Armstrong's birthplace in Wapakoneta, Ohio. I felt a swell of emotion begin to overtake me. I, too, wanted to be a part of something important, something larger than myself. I imagined space as my own frontier.

Scott at ten years old

First Man on the Moon, Neil A. Armstrong. Courtesy NASA

The next day, I persuaded my brother, Steve, to assist me on my first space mission. I confidently suited up in a plastic fire helmet and winter gloves and climbed into my makeshift capsule—the glass-front clothes dryer. Steve shut the door behind me. The fit was tight, and I felt claustrophobic. Then, to my surprise, Steve turned on the dryer! Fortunately, my flight was a brief one. One rotation and a couple bumps later, I banged on the door, and my brother reluctantly allowed my "splashdown." To this day, whenever I load clothes into a dryer, I have to shake off the uneasiness of that memory.

I was born on February 12, 1959, in Bryan, Ohio, but our family moved shortly thereafter about fifteen miles northwest to Montpelier, a small village in the northwestern corner of the state, covering a mere 2.7 square miles. Its claim to fame is a man named Paul Siple, who invented and coined the term "wind chill factor." He was also the first Boy Scout to earn the rank of Eagle

Scout. As a child, I dreamed of moving back to Bryan, where at least they had Ohio Art and its Etch A Sketch and Spangler Candy with all the Dum Dum suckers you could eat. Montpelier was divided down the middle by the Wabash train line. A train sped by daily, carrying new automobiles from Detroit to Chicago. If you were well-off, you lived on one side of the tracks; those not so well-off were on the other side. We lived right next to the tracks, on the "other" side.

Both of my parents were natives of Ohio. My father, Dick Phillips, was born in Toledo, the son of a paint-and-wallpaper business owner. My mother, Mary Lue Walker, was from Bryan, where her father worked for the telephone company before he started a television repair business with her brother Jack. Mom and Dad were high school sweethearts. Dad went on to attend Toledo University, where he participated in the ROTC program. They continued their relationship while Mom finished high school and Dad commuted to college. In 1954, Dad married my mother, and they spent their honeymoon in Niagara Falls. One year later, soon after my older sister Debbie was born, he joined the army with the rank of second lieutenant and they spent the next three years in Fort Lee, Virginia, before returning to Bryan.

My mother had always dreamed of continuing her education in nursing, but from an early age, she was discouraged by her father from having a career. Even I can recall my granddad saying many times, "A woman's place is in the home." So instead, she started a family right away, sacrificing her dreams as she gave birth to five children in less than seven years—Debbie, Steve, me, Lori, and Susan. Still, I often heard her pine, "If there was one thing I missed out on, it was pursuing my education to become a nurse."

The Phillips Family in 1967 (left to right: Scott,
Dad, Lori, Debbie, Mom, Steve, Susan)

Dad worked hard to provide for our family. He was a risk-taker,
accepting fresh opportunities with great energy and enthusiasm
in his relentless pursuit of success. He had majored in accounting,
but once he saw that sales was potentially more lucrative than
sitting behind a desk crunching numbers, he became a traveling
salesman. He worked on commission and frequently changed
employers. Of course, he was on the road a great deal and had
more downs than ups in his work. Dad was high strung, and he
dominated Mom's time when he was home. If he had a good
week of sales, he was happy, but after a bad week, Mom would
have to try to console him while keeping us kids at bay.

There was always an underlying sense of despair in the house.
My parents would often have conversations long into the night.
Their tone sometimes frightened me, and I imagined that I was
part of their problem. When that happened, I had the advantage
of being totally deaf in my right ear after a bout of rheumatic

fever as an infant. I would carefully nuzzle my good ear into the pillow and fall asleep.

All too often, there was more month left than there was money. My father struggled to provide a roof over our heads, somewhat reliable transportation, food on the table, and other basic necessities. Once, the water heater burned out, and it took two months to scrape up the money to replace the heating element. We boiled water on the stove for our baths.

Then there was the time Mom picked up Lori, Susan, and me from the community pool in our green '64 Chevy. It was a hot summer day and the windows were rolled down. As we crested the bridge over the railroad tracks, we heard a strange sound, like tumbling rocks against metal. As Mom accelerated, the noise became louder, and we felt the front-end shimmy. She applied the brakes, and to our astonishment, the right front wheel flew off. The car came to a sudden stop, but the wheel continued down the street. I hopped out of the car and ran after it. It jumped a curb into someone's front yard, and I grabbed for it, burning my hand in the process. As I was rolling the wheel back to the car, a newspaper reporter happened to be walking down the street and took a picture. We were rescued by a tow truck and learned that the bolts holding the lug nuts were rusted and had sheared off, ending up inside the hubcap. The next day, on the front page of the local paper, there was a picture of our car, with the front wheel missing and Mom clearly sitting in the driver's seat. Her usual sense of humor was nowhere to be found.

I didn't realize it at the time, but deep down, what Dad wanted most was to start his own business. All I knew was that he didn't bring home a steady paycheck and our family frequently picked up and moved. Mom always made the best of our circumstances and tried to make each place we lived a comfortable home. She let us pick paint colors for our rooms and thought of other ways to make us feel at ease and supported in our new surroundings.

She was so good at this that at one point, we were slow to realize that we lived in a haunted house.

We had been forced to move quickly when the house we had been renting was sold, and Dad mentioned our plight to a local realtor who owned the place. Apparently, he was having problems selling the property because the previous occupant had committed suicide in an upstairs bedroom. Dad was reluctant, but because he was in a pinch, he agreed to rent the place. He painted the blood-stained walls and moved us in.

It was a rather dilapidated old structure, built in the late 1800s. Even though we didn't know anything about the house or what had happened there, we soon felt there was something creepy about the place. A mysterious aura seemed to surround it, and we all had weird experiences, including—my sisters swore this was true—faces seeming to pop out from the upstairs walls. One night I was alone in the house, watching TV in my parents' bedroom, when an eerie sense crept over me. I made a beeline for the door and sat on the front lawn until everyone returned home.

Steve and I shared a bedroom on the main floor while everyone else slept upstairs. Our room was directly off the kitchen, next to the door leading to the dungeon-like basement we all actively avoided. At night, we would hear the pipes hum and chatter, and the sound of scratching engaged our imaginations with chilling thoughts of what was lurking behind the walls. In addition, the house sat behind the fire station, so it wasn't uncommon for us to be awakened in the middle of the night by screaming sirens. Once again, my hearing issue paid off. I trained myself to always go to sleep lying on my good ear.

We also learned that the house next door had once been a funeral home. As was customary at the time, the owners lived upstairs, the viewing parlors were on the main floor, and bodies were embalmed in the basement. Sometimes, we would look out our windows and wonder what was behind the only remnants of the original funeral home—the opaque crystallized basement windows. Then to make matters worse, we discovered that the current owner of that house had been convicted of murdering his wife's lover. Despite all of this, we lived in the home for almost three years.

When we were very young, Mom often worked temporary jobs to fill in the financial gaps, especially at Christmas when she wanted to be sure there would be plenty of gifts for each of us. But after my youngest sister, Susan, started school, Mom went to work full-time, mostly in factory jobs because they paid fairly well. For a while, Mom found employment at a local electronics manufacturer. From there, she went to work full-time at a nursing home. It didn't pay well, but it did help foster her passion for nursing and caring for others. She had amazing compassion for the clients, and families would often ask for her. She knew how to make people feel special. But Dad never understood her interest in the work and discouraged it, mostly due to the low pay. She got a good-paying job at a machine shop making cutting tools, but the work was difficult and the environment was harsh because of a high level of noise. When she'd get home, a heavy scent of oil lingered on her.

Wherever she worked, during the school year, she tried, as much as possible, to schedule her work hours so that we weren't home alone for long in the afternoons. Summer vacation was more problematic. I was still in grade school when Debbie, just twelve years old, had to move into the role of babysitter for the rest of us.

Some of my earliest memories are of Debbie in charge of us in our parents' absence. Even as a young girl, she was kind, generous, and considerate. A perfect example was the time she was selling fruitcakes as part of a school fund-raising project. After we located her stash in her closet, the cakes began disappearing one by one. Upon discovering that most of her inventory was gone, she gathered us together and asked, "Who took the fruitcakes?" After confirming that we were all involved, she quietly replaced them with her babysitting money. She never said another word to us—or to our parents.

This touches on a characteristic that was very important in our family. You know how families will have something that is totally forbidden, something that one could never commit without dire consequences? In our family, it was dishonesty. We were taught to always, always tell the truth. Despite the constant lectures, I had to learn this the hard way, and I'll never forget the lesson. One Saturday, Mom prepared a ham. She covered it with foil and placed it in the fridge, telling us, "I don't want anyone to touch this ham. It's for Sunday dinner." Then she and Dad left for a meeting, and we kids all went outside to play. A while later, I came in to get a snack. No one else was in the house, and I thought a ham sandwich sounded rather tasty. I got a knife and meticulously carved off several slices of ham and smothered them with mustard and pickles. I then carefully re-covered the ham and placed it back where Mom had put it.

Later that evening, my mom peeled back the foil and noticed the missing chunks of ham. "Who ate the ham?" she demanded. Dad chimed in, "And no lying!" Everyone, of course, denied any involvement. Since no one 'fessed up, all five of us were sent to our rooms—crying. I remember Lori screaming, "Whoever did it had better admit it!" But it had already gone too far at that point, and I felt committed to carrying out the lie. Dad yelled upstairs once more, "Confess and you can come down and eat dinner." When no one owned up to it, we had to go to bed without dinner. Still, at that point, I was thinking, *Yes! I got away with it!*

But in the middle of the night, I awoke feeling guilty. I had let everybody down and put my brother and sisters in a bad situation. I began to feel nauseated—until I couldn't hold it back any longer and tossed up the evidence. Mom came upstairs and said, "We found our culprit!" My dad later told me that he knew we all had consciences and that was why he pushed it. I apologized to my siblings, but I knew it would take time to earn back their trust.

From that point forward and to this very day, I have found it was much easier to just tell the truth.

The best memory of my family all together is from 1968. With the backdrop of the assassinations of Robert Kennedy and Martin Luther King, we packed up and headed to Washington, DC, for our one and only family vacation. Coming from a small town with limited "big city" opportunities, we were all giddy with excitement at the thought of staying in a hotel with a pool! As we drove through Pennsylvania, Dad turned his head and asked, "Anyone remember locking the door when we left?" Ooops! While no one remembered doing it, we kept going. It was a time—and place—that you could forget that sort of thing and everything would be all right. After a tour of the historical monuments, we visited Arlington National Cemetery. It was just a few weeks after Bobby Kennedy had been laid to rest and the mound of dirt was still fresh on his grave. I was overwhelmed with the thought of witnessing something this historical.

After our tour of the cemetery, we caught the open tram back to where our car was parked just as it started to rain. My mom was dying her hair black back in those days, and dark streaks started to run down her face. Dad quickly retrieved his handkerchief so she could wipe the mess from her face and cover her head to prevent further damage. We all thought it was hysterical, and Mom maintained her sense of humor through it all. We always appreciated that about her.

We piled back in our blue '64 Oldsmobile, which had been parked near the Washington Monument. As we were driving out of the city, the engine overheated and began spewing steam. As Dad lifted the hood, a kind black man came over and asked, "Is your car air-conditioned?" When my dad said no, the man took a toolbox from his vehicle and removed the thermostat. Dad thanked him profusely, and the car ran perfectly for the remainder of our vacation. During a time when our country was struggling with the pain of civil rights issues, the way that good-hearted stranger reached out to my family made a lasting impression on me. I constantly remind myself that everyone is the same and how it is important to respect and extend ourselves to people in need.

Because of our diverse personalities, managing our brood was a challenge, especially for Debbie during our parents' absence. For the most part, we all got along, but the words, "That's not fair!" were often heard; finding the balance of fairness was a constant battle. Mostly, it was the boys against the girls. Steve was an instigator that helped fuel the fire.

We all had chores during the day while our parents were at work: Steve was in charge of mowing the grass, I did the vacuuming, and the girls took care of cooking and maintaining the kitchen. Lori had a tendency to be sensitive. We would sometimes yank her chain just to get a reaction from her. One of my daily chores was to set the table for dinner. Selecting from our assortment of new and old silverware, I would purposely give Lori the old fork just to rankle her. It worked every time.

Susan was a tomboy and always loved animals. It seemed we were always taking in a new kitten or puppy. She was ecstatic when a neighbor gave her a small painted pony named Twinkles. The family next door offered a stall in their barn and every day—rain or shine—Susan made sure to feed, exercise, and change the straw in the stall. Twinkles had a mind of her own and would routinely bust out of her stall, prompting Susan to chase after her. We would hear her call for help, and after a few times, it became routine for all of us to run into the corn field to catch Twinkles. With the posse on her trail, we would always find her, and after a skillful lasso, one of us would trot her home safely. If I didn't know better, I would think Twinkles escaped just to give us some fun!

Despite her many other responsibilities, Debbie was also very involved in school activities. I looked up to her as a role model and was proud to follow her in school. When I started first grade,

I was very quiet and shy. This was especially true around girls, who I mostly avoided. At least until one day when our teacher announced, "There are two students who received 100 percent on the spelling test. Kelly and Scott, please stand up." That's when I first noticed Kelly, and I quickly developed a case of puppy love.

During summer vacation, Steve and I spent most of our days at the community pool. I would secretly watch for Kelly, who always wore a yellow and white bathing suit, and it would make my day when she showed up. This school-boy crush led to a big moment in my young life. The pool had a high-diving board, but before you were allowed to climb the ladder, you had to pass a difficult test: swimming the length of the pool three times. I had watched this process a number of times and was keenly aware that most kids failed on their first attempt. I thought if I passed the test on my first try, I might also win Kelly's heart. With her watching, failure was not an option. To this day, I'm not sure how I did it, but I did. It must have been a combination of determination mixed with a dose of testosterone. I felt I could accomplish anything that day.

I still had a crush on her in second grade, and one day, while sitting in music class, I wrote a love note in ink on the bottom of my shoe. I planned to hold up my shoe and show her at lunch. Just as I finished writing it, the teacher walked up and grabbed my shoe. She read the note and told me to clean it with the blackboard cleaner and a rag.

It wasn't until seventh grade that I got the nerve to ask Kelly to the movies. My class had received free passes, and she agreed to go with me along with a few other classmates. During the movie, she made comments and asked questions, but I didn't respond. She later asked me why. We realized that she had been sitting on the side of my deaf ear, and I hadn't heard her. The following year, she agreed to be my date for the eighth-grade graduation dance.

By the time I entered eighth grade, I had sprouted to almost six feet tall. One day as I was walking down the hall toward my locker, I noticed that the basketball coach had posted a signup sheet for a one-on-one basketball elimination as a way of determining the best players for the upcoming season. I entered the competition and talked my friend and tallest kid in the class, Lane Shoup, into entering as well.

There were twenty guys altogether, including a real hotshot player named Randy Fisher. Randy, Lane, and I all won our sets. After winning the next couple of rounds, Randy and I elevated to the top two spots—the final coveted one-on-one. With a few seconds to go, we were tied, and I decided to go for it. I dribbled underneath the net and threw the ball behind my back and—to my amazement—made the winning shot! Randy started to cry. I think it blew his mind that he lost. I still have the gold medal that I was awarded.

One-on-One Gold medal

Naturally, the three of us were selected for the team. Even though we were initially competitors, after several weeks of practice, we came together as the first string players. On the day of our first game, it was tradition that the players all wore neckties to build team spirit. We were strutting our stuff at lunch, and I was carrying my tray past the cheerleaders and wondered why they were all laughing at me. When I sat down and placed my tray on the table, I noticed that my tie was floating in my tomato soup. As I dabbed it with a napkin, I had to admit it was rather funny and shared a laugh with my teammates. We then quickly turned our thoughts and conversation toward the excitement of our home game after school, which would be played under the threat of a severe snowstorm. Unfortunately, we lost but took solace in knowing we had the whole season ahead of us.

After the game, I quickly showered and pulled my sweat pants over my gym shorts and threw on a sweatshirt over my tank top. I lived about three miles from school, and normally, Lane's mother would give me a ride home. I hadn't worn my winter jacket that day because I was expecting to have a ride home. But in the parking lot, Lane told me his mom couldn't give me a ride that night. I glanced back to the gym door and realized I was the last guy out and the school had been locked tight. I looked up at the single light above the door and saw snowflakes swirling around it. It was around 6:00 p.m. and already dark. The final cars pulled out of the parking lot, and I was standing there alone.

All of a sudden, it seemed like a ghost town. I had no phone to call my family, and the storm was moving in fast. I could see my breath as I made a split-second decision to jog the three miles home.

I had gone about a mile when the flurries quickly changed to an all-out blizzard. I came to a crossroad, where I could go the long way around by following the roads or I could cut across the plowed field straight to my house. I could faintly see the night light coming from the pole barn next to our house and decided the detour would be faster. Halfway through the field, I came to a creek. I miscalculated the distance and landed in the icy water. I pulled a semi-wet towel from my gym bag and tried to dry myself. My shoes were soaked, and I was shivering violently. As I crouched on my knees with fatigue, it was snowing so hard I could barely see my guiding light. My ears, fingers, and toes ached, and I felt a strong urge to lay my head down on my gym bag. But I knew that if I did that, as tired as I was, I might fall asleep and would soon be covered with a foot of snow. *They might not find me until the spring*, I thought in horror. A small voice deep inside me said, "Get up! Keep moving!" Somehow, I made it safely home. My siblings had been concerned that I was late, but they just assumed Mrs. Shoup had been delayed by the snow. I never shared the real details with my family. It was a pivotal lesson, and I left some of my childhood innocence behind that night. From that point on, I always took responsibility for my decisions and actions—right or wrong.

That night and its meaning would come back to me years later during my "Mudman" experience in the Space Shuttle's external liquid oxygen tank.

For a while, Dad recruited students for a girls' finishing school out of Fort Wayne, Indiana. He went door-to-door selling to families with high school seniors. The one-year, prepaid program included classes on home economics, business, and etiquette. We kids referred to it as the Beauty School. It went well for a couple years until a disgruntled father demanded his money back. He had prepaid his daughter's tuition and halfway through the program she lost interest. Dad had closed the sale, so his name was on the contract, and the man came to the school demanding to see Dick Phillips. Dad happened to be in his office at the time, and the man tried to intimidate him, saying, "I want my money back or I'm going to kick your ——!"

This rattled Dad. He stopped on the way home to visit my mom's brother Tom, a gun collector, and borrowed a .22 caliber, single-shot, lever-action rifle. He loaded it and secured it in his bedroom closet in case the man showed up at our house. Dad admonished us not to open the door to strangers and to keep the screen door locked. It was the type of experience you never forget. Fortunately, nothing happened, but the episode soured Dad on the Beauty School and sales—for a while. Accounting was not his preferred field, but he accepted a temporary position with an automotive manufacturing company in Bryan, but only with the promise of a transfer to the sales department when a spot opened.

During my early school years, I was blessed with several mentors who recognized and nurtured my creative gifts. One of my early influences came into my life because of one of my chores. Dad wore wing-tipped shoes with thick soles, a necessity for a salesman. When the shoes needed to be resoled, as they often did, I had to deliver them to Mr. Siebenaler, our local cobbler. His shop was in the basement of a downtown building. It felt like I was walking into a mineshaft, as only one small window faced the stairway leading down. Upon entering his shop, I was greeted by a tinkling bell and the welcoming aroma of leather and shoe polish. The front counter was very high, like a deli case, with newly repaired shoes lining the top. I would watch as Mr. Siebenaler tagged Dad's shoes and staged them for repair. A week later, I'd retrieve the transformed shoes. Dad was always happy when I came home with his "new" shoes. I would watch as he wore them for the first time, and I swear I saw an extra spring in his step.

Mr. Siebenaler and I never shared a conversation, but that quiet, friendly man introduced me to the idea of turning something old into something new as I witnessed craftsmanship at its finest. What was truly inspiring was to watch him create prosthetic devices. I went to school with his daughter, Margo, and there were several of our fellow students who wore leg braces and orthotic devices he had made for their physical conditions. My contact with Mr. Siebenaler touched the inventor, the innovator, and the renovator in me.

Montpelier Shoe Cobbler, Mr. Siebenaler

Another guide was my elementary school art teacher, Mrs. Juanita Shatzer. She was a bit flamboyant and passionate about working with kids. I always looked forward to art class. It provided an outlet for my creative expression. With what seemed to be unlimited tools and supplies readily available for my projects, I felt energized. I remember a class project of designing and building an Indian reservation. I was tasked with creating the teepees out of leather sheets. I worked hard to make them as realistic as possible. When I finished, Mrs. Shatzer smiled and said, "Scotty, you did such a wonderful job on the teepees." Those simple words of encouragement fueled my confidence. I was always proud when parents came to school to see our projects displayed on the walls. I later learned that Mrs. Shatzer had studied to be a social worker, but when an opening came up for an art teacher at Montpelier Primary, she instantly knew that was her true calling.

Montpelier Elementary Art Teacher, Juanita Shatzer

She once gave my family an old dresser that was in rather poor condition, and Mom said, "Hey, Scott, see what you can do with this." The drawers were stuck shut and the handles were tarnished. I turned it upside down to remove the drawers, stripped the wood clean, and discovered it was solid walnut. I remade the drawer runners and applied a fresh coat of clear lacquer. I cleaned the handles with a wire brush and then polished and restored them to their original condition. To this day, it's a beautiful addition in my home and serves as a tangible reminder of the inspiration and encouragement I received from Mrs. Shatzer.

I became my family's go-to guy for repairing or building just about anything. I recall a vacuum cleaner that continued to go on the fritz. I repaired it so many times that the cord would reach only a few feet. Even though it was beyond repair at that point, I took the responsibility and felt bad for letting my family down, a feeling I strongly disliked.

I loved to tinker. I didn't have any sophisticated tools, but if I had a need or an idea, I'd find a way to make it happen—often to my mother's consternation. Once I searched the utensil drawer until I found the meat saw, which I used to cut up her broom and mop handles for whittling projects. That was where I gained my energy. I felt empowered and energized when I figured out a solution to a problem, and I needed a pathway to channel this passion.

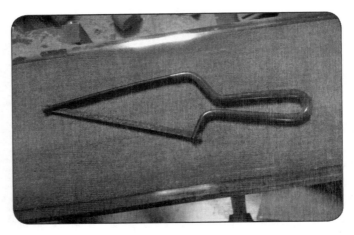

Our vintage meat saw

My mom's youngest brother, Jack, also liked to work with wood. I was inspired by him. Because of his woodworking skills and TV repair business, I thought Uncle Jack could fix just about anything. He was always in the middle of some project. I remember wishing I could just hang out with him, but that wasn't always possible because he lived too far away to walk and he was busy with his own family. He and my granddad were both woodworkers, so I guess you could say my passion for woodworking came naturally. When Uncle Jack heard about how I was using Mom's kitchen utensils as tools, he gave me a saber saw with a miniature turning lathe.

Uncle Jack Walker

I could hardly believe I finally owned my very first woodworking tools. I couldn't wait to get home to use them. After carefully setting it up in the dirt-floored basement, I realized there was no access to power. I looked around the basement and found several old lamps. I thought, *I can connect the lamp wires and use it as an extension cord!* I had no tools, but I refused to be defeated. Using a steak knife, I spliced the wires, connected the plugs, and bound the lengths together with Scotch tape. Fortunately, it was long enough to reach all the way from the kitchen down the stairs to my lathe. My invention worked and the thought of it being a potential fire hazard never crossed my mind. The saw blade turned out to be dull, but I didn't care. I just worked harder to get my results. I learned that I could sharpen a screwdriver on concrete with sandpaper and use it as the cutting mechanism on the lathe. It produced crude turnings but provided me with the ability and confidence to accurately center materials. I was so excited to start making things, but I needed more wood. Once again, I went back in search of Mom's meat saw and cut some limbs off the trees in our yard. They were adequate, but I decided Mom's broom handles had worked much better.

No one showed me how to use the equipment, and I spent hours and hours learning how to turn wood. My projects were unsuccessful at first, but I spent an entire summer perfecting my turning skills. When I returned to school in the fall, I was excited to take my projects and show my science and art teacher.

Scott with family dog, Kippy

Because we moved around so much, my siblings became my closest friends and biggest influences, especially my brother Steve. During the summers in Montpelier, he and I made weekly trips to the appliance store to gather sturdy boxes for sliding down the hill from the top of the viaduct alongside the train tracks. The underside of the box would become shiny and wildly slippery after only a few runs. We called it box skiing. At the bottom of our ride was a fenced high-powered substation with an ominous sign warning, "33,000 Volts! Danger!" The thrill of the slide was to see how close we could get to the fence without hitting it. That number always stuck in my mind, and the number 33 became significant later in my career.

In the winter, Steve and I would play the same game except we would use a 30-inch aluminum disk with handles over the snow. One day, we got creative and constructed a long curved ramp out of snow at the foot of the hill to launch us into the air. We were eager to try out our invention with our new red disk, and as we discussed the potential risks, we spotted a classmate watching us. Jerry Munson was an unpopular kid, somewhat of an outcast. Steve waved him over, yelling, "Hey, Munson. Try out our new ride!" He came over, and surprisingly, he was eager to try it.

With the disk in hand, he trudged up to the top of the hill and prepared for his big ride. We figured there was only a 50/50 chance it would work without him tumbling over the side or picking up too much speed and landing in the fence—but at least, we didn't have to test it ourselves! Munson positioned himself on the disk and pushed off. What happened next was beyond our wildest dreams. He sailed down the hill, and when he hit the end of the ramp, we heard a shrill scream as he did a complete 360-degree, midair flip. As we retrieved his limp body, we were relieved to see that he had only suffered a busted lip. From the amount of blood-stained snow, we thought it was much worse. He was missing his eyeglasses and we found them mangled next to the fence. We walked him home to make sure he was all right.

As we entered his front door, we noticed that there was no carpet. In fact, there wasn't even any flooring. Munson's house had dirt floors. At that moment, I felt grateful—at least we had carpeting in our house. We returned to the ramp and remorsefully removed it so no one else could get hurt. What was intended to be an innocent childhood game taught me that folly can have serious consequences.

Steve and I had very different temperaments, and we fought a lot. I always felt that he thought it was his job to toughen me up and test my mettle. For several years, we lived in the country just outside of Montpelier on an acre of land with several apple trees on the property. One day, Steve and I decided to use the overripe fruit that had fallen in the yard for a fight. We filled two garbage can lids with the rotten apples, and when we had enough ammunition, we marked our respective territories and began throwing them like baseballs. About thirty minutes into our battle, Steve hit me square in the eye. As the juice ran down my face, he shouted, "I win!" Not wanting to admit defeat, I yelled back, "Oh no, you didn't. I'm not finished!" Damned if he didn't throw another one straight into my other eye! I went to school the next day with two black eyes. He was relentless.

Some of my greatest summertime memories are of Steve and I renting a tandem bike. Steve had a substitute newspaper route, and he used his own money to rent the bike. We would walk to the local ACE hardware store in downtown Montpelier, and he would treat us to a one-hour rental. We quickly learned there was a big difference between riding and steering. The bicycle chains are connected, and it forces you to keep the same timing. We would switch on and off steering until we learned to trust ourselves and each other in this role.

Once we were comfortable with the mechanics, we concocted a game out of it by having the person in the back close his eyes while the person in front steered to an unknown destination. The rider was required to calculate the turns and distances to accurately determine the location. We would start at the hardware store and stop at the post office to regroup before going into the neighborhoods. Steve would have thirty minutes and then it would be my turn. The one rule was that you could not peek, which naturally amplified all our other senses. I could tell by the fragrance of pine when we were near wooded areas and could sense by the sounds and the smells when we were close to the St. Joseph River. I felt the sensation of every turn, every bump, and every water puddle we splashed through. Most of the time we would squeal, "Yeehaw!" but invariably, I would also have to holler, "Slow down! You're going too fast!" It was all about two brothers learning to trust each other. It was exhilarating going downhill—blindly—knowing we had each other's backs. The sensation was similar to riding a roller coaster in the dark. My calculations were correct most of the time; no doubt, this was early training for my intuitive senses, which have served me well throughout my life and career.

When we kids were older, we would find ways to make financial contributions to the family. When she was sixteen, Debbie got a job at a radio station and the local newspaper. It helped to launch a passion for journalism that would serve her well later. And as soon as they were old enough to handle the responsibility, Lori and Susan earned money by babysitting children in the neighborhood.

Steve was ambitious and hardworking, and nearby farms were always in need of extra hands baling hay and doing pasture work, although the pay was low. I was still a preteen, but Steve always included me when he negotiated for jobs. That's where I first learned about hard work—baling hay. During the summer, we worked on the Clemons family farm and lived with them for entire weeks at a time. The long days produced blisters and achy muscles, but we looked forward to the home-cooked meals. Unfortunately, on many days, the roofs of our mouths would be so sore from all the dust that it was difficult to get food down.

Farmer Clemons also had two daughters: Sharon and Karen. Karen was Steve's age and liked to flirt with the boys. She had a horse named Flicka, and as we worked, we would watch her ride. I was in the barn one day when Karen was saddling Flicka, and she asked, "Would you like to ride my horse?" I said, "Sure!" I had barely settled into the saddle when Flicka reared up and threw me off. I landed in brier bushes. The pain was intense, but I didn't want to make an awkward situation worse, so I got hold of the reins and we walked Flicka back to the barn without a word.

As Karen tended to the other horses, I sat on a hay bale nursing my wounds. A short while later, she came over and sat next to me. She looked at me, and I looked back into her sparkling blue eyes. To my shock and total surprise, she planted a kiss on my lips. My first kiss. Then she jumped up and took off running. I chased after her and tackled her into a nearby hay bale where I planted a return kiss on her lips. I felt drawn to the excitement of her body next to mine, yet scared and confused at the same time. Just then her mother hollered, "Get back to work baling hay!" It was the last day of the season, and I never saw her again. But the memory of that first kiss lingered for a long, long time.

There was the one major incident with Steve in which the two of us failed to follow the family rule about honesty, and we were lucky that we lived to tell about it—although we did keep the secret for decades. Living in the country provided little entertainment. So it was fortunate when Steve was finally old enough to drive. He saved his money and purchased a '64 Chevy. He and I would make the three-mile trip to town whenever we needed to pick something up for Mom or if we were just bored.

One rainy night, we announced to our parents, "We're heading into town for pizza." The real reason for the trip was that Steve wanted to have a cigarette—something our parents would not approve of. Steve slid into the driver's seat and buckled his lap belt. I was so excited to be tagging along that I entered the passenger's side without giving any thought to the seatbelt.

It was his first trip into town after he had been on a weeklong vacation to Florida with his girlfriend and her family. That night, as he turned the radio volume full throttle, I noticed he had a devious expression on his face. Steve was driving fast on the country roads as he reached under the seat and brought out a small bag. With a sly grin, he said, "Look what I bought on the drive back from Florida." He pulled out what looked like firecrackers. He grabbed a bottle rocket, ignited the short fuse with his cigarette, and flung it out of his window. It shot wildly into the air and exploded behind us. As he accelerated even faster, he lit another and pitched it out the window. This one landed in the nearby cornfield and detonated. I rolled my window down, saying, "Let me try one!" Eager to continue the excitement, he held out his lit cigarette and I ignited the fuse.

By this time, we were going at least eighty miles an hour. As I tossed the lit bottle rocket out the window, the wind caught it and whirled it back into the car and landed in the backseat. After an ominous hissing sound, it exploded. Steve panicked, and as he took his eyes off the road to assess the damage, the right front wheel dropped off into the muddy berm, causing him to oversteer to regain control. He jerked the wheel to get back on the road; it didn't take much at the speed we were going to cause us to cross the centerline and send us straight into an adjacent cornfield. I closed my eyes as we left the road and became nauseated. Shock quickly overtook me, but my senses were vivid. I felt the car rocking and rolling and heard the crunching of metal and the popping sound of shattering glass. It felt like an eternity as my body moved through the interior of the car. The car rolled twice and came to an abrupt stop upside down in the field. Steve was suspended upside down by his seatbelt, and I ended up in the back window. The car was still running and the radio blared a Led Zeppelin tune. I smelled an overpowering odor of gasoline, and I intuitively yelled, "Turn the engine off!" The top of the car was smashed and the windshield was shattered. The doors were jammed shut, and we had to crawl through a narrow space in the open window on the passenger's side.

After regaining our senses and realizing we were all right, we decided I would stay with the car, and Steve, guided only by the bright headlights, walked to the farmhouse a quarter mile away to call Dad. He soon returned and shared the details of his quickly concocted story. "Dad's coming to get us," he said. "I told him that a deer ran out in front of us and I lost control." I said nothing, and when Dad came, I let Steve do the talking. It seemed like the least I could do. Even though we sustained only minor cuts and bruises, we stayed home from school the next day. But the following day, as the school bus passed our upside-down car in the cornfield, we were told that everyone had thought we were seriously injured—or worse.

We kept our secret for many years in spite of Dad's suspicions that there was more to the story. Steve later shared with me that he experienced reoccurring dreams that I didn't survive the accident. "I thought I had killed you," he said. Even though he liked to pick on me, that spoke volumes of his love and genuine concern. Several decades later, he told me that he finally recanted the deer story and told Dad what actually happened. I didn't press for details, and my dad never spoke of it with me.

Dad's entrepreneurial spirit could not be contained. Always on the lookout for new opportunities, in the early '70s, my parents answered an ad about an innovative start-up business in Angola, Indiana, called Amway. They jumped at the opportunity and started hosting meetings in our home on Friday nights. Dad presented the opportunity and Mom demonstrated the products. Within a year, they had built a solid business and realized a fairly significant profit. Dad saw a future for our family in Amway. And since the sales job at the manufacturing company was still on hold, he resigned his accounting position and began directing his energies full time toward Amway.

While things were looking up financially, the downside was that our parents had to travel a lot in order to grow their business. They were often asked to speak at meetings and give their testimony—at their expense—with the hope that it would promote sales. In the early days, company representatives had to maintain their own inventory and products were hand delivered.

For three years, our family was motivated by success stories of other families, and we saw what the business could mean for us. We kids eagerly participated by loading and unloading materials and stocking products in our utility room, oftentimes carrying 100-pound boxes of laundry soap. Steve and I would accompany my dad whenever he drove the ninety miles north to Ada, Michigan, to pick up products from the Amway warehouse. We were excited when our parents were asked to speak at a meeting in Fort Wayne, Indiana, sixty miles away and the whole family was going along. Plus, the meeting was to be at a brand-new Marriott, which had an indoor swimming pool!

My dad had been a smoker for about twenty years—ever since his military days. A couple weeks before the trip, Dad experienced a collapsed lung. He was rushed to the hospital where he stayed for ten days. It was almost an entire year before he fully recovered. Without his constant involvement, the business failed. My parents painfully realized that they had recruited people who were left adrift without Dad at the helm. Saddled with disappointment and health issues, my dad was forced back into the job market. Opportunities were scarce in Montpelier at the time, so he, once again, reached out in the Fort Wayne area. He answered an ad and accepted a position selling cemetery properties. Little did he know that this opportunity was the first rung of a long climb to his eventual success and making his dream come true.

> *Woodism*
>
> *Individuals who recognize God's gifts will share
> in life's possibilities and unseen beauty*

Southern Migration

In 1974, Dad accepted a job in Florence, Alabama, managing and revitalizing a neglected cemetery park that had gone into bankruptcy. Although we had moved frequently over the years, we had never left the area near the northern border of Ohio and Indiana. This would be a major disruption for our family, but Dad was eager for the challenge and embraced the opportunity.

My parents were invited to visit Alabama before making their final decision to move, and they returned with tantalizing stories of the Tennessee River with boating, water skiing, picnic grounds, warm weather, and great barbecue. It sounded like a resort to us! We joked about moving to the South and taking up a new accent, saying things like "y'all" and "over yonder."

It was a time of change in our family dynamics as well. Debbie had finished high school and moved to Columbus after she earned multiple scholarships to Ohio State University. We were proud and happy for her, but we were losing the considerable day-to-day support and inspiration she brought to our family.

Steve moved with us to Alabama, but within a few months, at eighteen, he joined the army. He didn't tell anyone of his plans. He went down to the recruiting office, signed up, and was gone within a couple months. Dad was happy to see him follow in his footsteps, and we all saw it as a great opportunity for Steve. But he and I had developed a special bond during our teen years. When he left, I felt abandoned. I had lost my friend and cohort in crime. He was stationed in Germany for three years, with only two 30-day leaves home during that time.

We immediately fell in love with the South. I tasted my first southern barbecue—not like the minced version up North—and quickly took a liking to sweet tea, grits, and cornbread. People were friendly but curious. Classmates wanted to hear our Northern accents. "Talk Yankee for us!" they'd beg. People were a bit guarded since we represented the North. We would jokingly hear things like, "A happy Southerner is seeing a Yankee headed north on a bus!" We occasionally saw bumper stickers with the same sentiment.

The cemetery where Dad worked was a 50-acre property located on the main street going into the city of Florence. It had paved roads lined with trees and was divided into five sections with names like "Everlasting Life," "Apostle's Garden," and "Gethsemane Garden." Dad saw the job as a long-term commitment with an opportunity for developing a mausoleum program. He had known that the property had been bankrupted and was in a state of neglect, but he didn't realize that it was also riddled with corruption, embezzlers, and racism. Dad was given the responsibility of making changes to the staff, revitalizing the neglect, and bringing civility to the business.

The perpetual care fund had been raided, and physically, the property was in total disrepair. The roads were deteriorated with potholes, statues and markers were crumbling, and the shrubbery was sparse and needed to be replaced. It appeared that the only maintenance being performed was grass mowing. The office needed a new roof and painting, and the logbook was old, and the equipment and furniture was outdated.

Our family jumped in and started working to renovate the office. Mom made curtains and we refinished the floors. Dad decided to brighten the walls with a soft shade of orange to make it more comfortable for the grieving families. He also bought a new flag and started the practice of raising it on the flagpole every day.

Everywhere Dad turned, he found fraud and corruption. At one time, the cemetery staff made concrete vaults with a steel mold reinforced with metal rebar, and families were charged a nominal fee for this product. But over the years, the local funeral directors began selling steel vaults, for which they charged families four times as much, and they paid the cemetery employees not to make the concrete vaults. The cemetery home office was not aware that staff was pocketing kickbacks. When Dad learned about this practice, he restarted making the vaults at the cemetery, angering the funeral directors. He then took on the issue of used flower sprays—a little side business that had been going on for twenty-five years. After an internment, the caretaker would pluck the flowers off the Styrofoam, clean the racks, and dip them in green paint. The racks would then be sold back to the florists and resold to new customers. The caretaker and receptionist had been enjoying a cushy non-taxable slush fund from this for years. Dad fired the entire staff.

Correcting the corruption and decay was challenging enough, but Dad also found out that part of his assignment was to racially integrate the cemetery. In the interim, as Dad looked to hire workers, Mom helped with his efforts to advertise to minorities. This raised new problems. Plots had been purchased on a pre-need basis, and once people found out that the cemetery had opened up to this new market, local businesses tried to incite the property owners and many of them then demanded refunds. In addition, we learned about the Ku Klux Klan, which was alive and well in the Florence area. We received threatening phone calls at home.

Dad became a member of the local Better Business Bureau, and many of the businesspeople were also members of the KKK. Dad was shunned for integrating the cemetery. When a local business owner who was a member of both groups and a vocal proponent of the protest suddenly died, he was buried in his prepaid plot next to his family members. There were a number of available plots close by his grave, and Dad sold them to minority families.

Hiring new staff was a challenge for a wide range of reasons. One man walked several miles to interview for the caretaker position. Unfortunately, he didn't have a Social Security number, so Dad was unable to hire him. Another guy, Bob, assured Dad that he had thirty years of experience in maintaining property. Dad met him over lunch and thought he had found the right person. But as Bob was leaving, his car was rear-ended at a nearby intersection. He unsuccessfully sued Dad's company on the basis that he was on a job interview when it happened.

Finally, Dad interviewed a fun-loving country boy who liked to tinker and rebuild machinery. This jack-of-all-trades was exactly what Dad needed for his maintenance supervisor. We all liked Ray. He told me he had been driving since he was nine but never had a driver's license. He liked Dad and was a loyal and devoted employee, remaining at the cemetery until his retirement.

When I turned sixteen, Dad hired me during the summer to haul dirt and mow grass. I enjoyed the independence that came from a paycheck, and driving the tractor reminded me of summers on the Clemons farm baling hay with Steve. I was supervised by Ray, who noted that I tended to be a bit of a hotshot on the tractor and constantly admonished me to slow down. Sure enough, one day as I was mowing grass, a bee flew in my eye and I t-boned a tree. Ray ran over, saying, "I told you that you were going too fast."

My first day on the job

One of my tasks was to prepare the plots by removing the grass and topsoil. I used an axe to score a rectangular line to break and loosen the sod. I hadn't really noticed until then how different the ground was from the rich black dirt in Ohio. In Alabama, there were clumps of sticky red clay. The summers were much hotter than I was used to, and I had to spend several hours almost every day clearing plots. I didn't like to refer to my job as gravedigger, but that was what I did.

I was active in the youth group at church, and that is where I met Janet. Her father had died and her mother remarried our minister. Janet was in a high school sorority and sort of a Southern belle, and it took me about six months to gather the courage to ask her on a date. She replied matter-of-factly, "I don't date guys who work at cemeteries." I was humiliated. That turned me off to the local girls, and I never asked another one out.

To keep my mind from thinking about the end result of my work, I would let my thoughts and imagination wander. I began to strategize practical jokes to lighten up the somber environment.

I remembered a practical joke I had played in sixth-grade science class when I shared a lab table with a girl I had a crush on. I got the crazy idea to fill a test tube with ammonia and pretended to take a deep whiff of it. I told her that it smelled like roses and invited her to try. To my horror, she took a much deeper whiff than I expected, and her eyes rolled back into her head, and she hit the floor—out cold! I sprinkled water on her face and she came to, but I was sick to my stomach about hurting someone. I suppose I got off lightly that I was merely sent home for the day. I vowed to myself to think through such plans a little better going forward, and I became quite proud of the level to which I could plan and execute practical jokes.

I devised what I thought would be a perfect prank to play on my father. As park manager, before a burial service, he would inspect the grave site to make sure everything was properly prepared—chairs were in place, the tent was set up correctly, and finally, the grave itself was ready. So one day, I jumped into the hole and laid on my back with my arms folded over my chest. It was a beautiful day, and I watched puffy white clouds glide across the sky as I patiently waited, like a fox anticipating its prey. I heard Dad's footsteps coming across the grass and chairs being moved around. It became quiet. I knew he'd soon look into the hole, and I prepared to scream, "Boo!" I saw his face appear above me, but before I could utter a sound, he wet his pants. His hand went over his mouth, and to this day, I'm not sure if he was stifling a scream or repositioning his dentures.

Dad had to lead the funeral in his soiled clothing—and I had to walk the three miles home that evening. He didn't speak to me for two weeks. It took a long time for the anger to fade, and I realized the embarrassing position I had put him in and the seriousness of how my practical joke could have turned out. But the "incident," as it would become known in the family, eventually took on a humorous life of its own. In fact, Dad later told the story at my wedding rehearsal dinner—many, many years later.

There never seemed to be a dull moment in the cemetery business. While I was working there, a man who had buried his wife a year earlier decided to retire and move to Arizona. He requested that his wife be exhumed so that he could reinter her in a burial site in his new location. The request was coordinated through a local funeral director, and it was a new and unique challenge for Dad, reversing a familiar process. The cemetery was on the main thoroughfare into town, and the plot was only about fifty yards back, well within sight of the road. The plan was to discretely exhume the body prior to daybreak to avoid curious onlookers. Dad decided to use existing equipment with minimal personnel. I was selected to be on the team with Mr. Peck, our backhoe driver, and Ray. Assuming the process would take a couple hours, we started promptly at 4:00 a.m.

My job was to lay the grave out by removing the sod, as I had done many times before. With my ax, I easily peeled back the sod squares that had been laid just one year prior. We had to work with speed and intention because daylight was fast approaching. Dad and I waited patiently as Mr. Peck moved in with his backhoe and removed the remaining dirt. As soon as he skimmed the top of the vault, I jumped in. I carefully dug with a trowel to reach the vault, exposing the corners. I was handed a cable and placed it around all four corners under the vault lip. Ray then positioned the vault trailer, straddling the grave opening, and lowered the chain from the block and tackle pulley about six feet overhead. Spread out over the vault, I attached the pulley hook to the center cable that held the corners of the vault. When the hook was securely fastened, Ray attempted to manually lift the vault with the block and tackle. It had been raining off and on all night and the weight of the vault and the suction from the red clay muck around and below the vault caused the pulley system to seize up. We were losing precious time. There we stood, with daylight approaching, in view of the morning traffic, attempting to dig up a body in the rain. Dad decided to make a second attempt using the backhoe. Mr. Peck found a heavy-duty chain and tied it around the backhoe digger, hoping that the vehicle's hydraulic system would be more successful. Unfortunately, the backhoe shut down due to a leak in the hydraulic line.

Dad refused to be discouraged. He called a local trucking company that owned a boom capable of lifting a twenty-ton truck. He raised the owner out of bed, and I could hear him on the other end of the line, "You've got to be kidding me! You want me to do what?" Dad said, "I'm dead serious. I'll pay you one hundred dollars cash." That was premium pay back in the '70s, and the man agreed.

Prior to his arrival, we had to remove over one hundred tombstone vases to allow room for his massive vehicle. The monster truck arrived just as the morning traffic hit. The sun was peeking through the clouds, and we were now totally exposed. Cars started slowing down. People were gawking and honking their horns. There was no tent, no flowers, no chairs, and the evidence clearly pointed to the fact we were exhuming a body. Someone notified the police, and they soon arrived on the scene as well. We had forgotten to alert the local authorities. We suffered a little embarrassment, but fortunately, no citation was rendered. With the boom in place, the vault was easily lifted. The driver was noticeably shaken about the job, and after Dad paid him, he left without saying a word. Once the vault was removed, exposing the casket, Ray returned with the trailer. I reentered the hole and placed straps around the head and the foot of the casket, hooked it to the chain, and the block and tackle pulley easily lifted the casket out and onto the trailer.

The funeral director was present to verify the serial number and contents. Dad turned to me and asked, "Is this something you would like to witness? Do you want to see the skeleton?" I was reluctant at first, but the science guy in me said, "Yes, I would." I was interested in seeing how a body decomposes. The casket was transferred to the ground by the pulley system and carefully positioned with the opening away from public view. The funeral director unlocked the casket and lifted the lid. I anticipated seeing a zombie, horror-like scene, but instead saw an individual who was powdery white without any facial features. It sort of looked like a Styrofoam manikin used to hold wigs. The nails were long and yellowed, and the hair and clothing showed signs of mold. We were surprised to find no odor. I found the experience very scientific and not at all creepy as I had originally imagined. I was impressed with how straightforward and matter-of-factly it was handled.

After completing his paperwork, the funeral director closed and locked the lid, and we all helped carry the casket to the waiting hearse. Ray and I looked at each other, realizing that, since the backhoe was out of commission, our day was just getting started. After removing the vault base, we spent the rest of the day filling in the hole with shovels. It was an interesting few years, and the tow truck driver and Dad became a local folk story at the trucking company. The biggest lesson I learned working with my dad at the cemetery—which served me well later in my career—is that no matter how well you plan, expect the unexpected.

I took driver's education in tenth grade. Our school was unique in that it had a driving range. Students spent one week in the classroom and one week on the range. We even had sports cars available—Firebirds, Camaros, and Thunderbirds. Students drove through the range alone as instructors communicated via two-way radios.

I liked a cute girl in the class and wanted to impress her with how cool I was. On one particular day, she was assigned a Thunderbird, and of all the luck, I ended up with a Dodge Dart. But there she was next to me in her candy-apple red sports car. I was first to start the drills, and I was totally focused on impressing this girl. I glanced over at her with the intent of peeling off. I adjusted my seat, checked my mirror, and noticed that she was looking at me. I looked at her, and as I reached down to release the brake, I mistakenly opened the hood. As I sat there with my face turning bright red, I heard the instructor razz me over the intercom, "Way to go, Phillips!" I sheepishly exited my vehicle and lowered the hood. The girl, the object of my infatuation, regarded me as if I were a moron as she drove past. Although I went on to ace the class, my humiliations were not over.

Dad and I went to the license bureau in our Kingswood Estate station wagon with a 400 HP engine. The examiner got in the car, and I was passing the test with ease. I had been driving a tractor and trailer most of the summer at the cemetery, so even parallel parking with a station wagon was a breeze. Everything was going smoothly, and as my excitement mounted, I murmured under my breath, "Freedom, here I come!" But as I pulled through the final intersection, a kid dashed out of the corner market and ran straight into my car, knocking him to the curb. I slammed on the brakes, and we rushed to check on him. An ambulance was called, and fortunately, the boy was not injured. "What happens now?" I asked. "Well, it's an automatic fail when something like this happens," the examiner said. I had to wait six long agonizing months to be retested and then damned if I didn't get the same evaluator. "Oh, it's you again," he said. I was well into my seventeenth year when I finally got my driver's license.

I was still a preteen when I first began to develop an interest in guitars from my mom's Sears catalogs. As soon as a new catalog arrived, I would open to the guitar section. I was captivated by the different shapes and varieties of woods, and I dreamed of playing the guitar. I was amazed that such a beautiful sounding instrument could be made out of wood. While I was working summers at the cemetery, I saved enough money and bought a red Guild guitar I had my eye on.

For the next two years, I took private lessons in downtown Florence. Daryl, my guitar teacher, was in his early twenties and of German descent. He was a brilliant guitarist but rather stoic and klutzy at the same time. I remember him telling me about the time he took a girl out on their first date. He said, "I flipped the car upside down and she broke her neck." Fortunately, the girl recovered, but it ended their relationship. He was a real character. I enjoyed playing guitar and learned to compensate for my hearing issue by feeling the vibrations on the guitar. My visual and mechanical skills gave me the confidence to learn. And because most of my free time was spent working, it also filled a loneliness in my life from not having made any close friends in Alabama.

We lived near the Muscle Shoals Sound, and I felt right at home with the likes of Percy Sledge, Lionel Richie, Neil Sedaka, Mac Davis, and Florence native, W. C. Handy, "Father of the Blues." Dad would occasionally drive us to the studio to see the display of gold records and awards in the lobby. We were always on the lookout for famous singers and our eyes widened whenever we saw limos, Jaguars, oversized busses, and even a Rolls Royce or two. The Muscle Shoals music industry was mainly country and blues, but I grew to really appreciate music listening to Debbie's records at home of Neil Young and James Taylor. My main influence and inspiration came from John Denver. His music inspired me.

Dad did everything he set out to do at the memorial park, including starting a mausoleum program. In fact, the turnaround was so successful that he eventually worked himself out of a job. He was transferred back to the home office in Indiana to take on a new project. We had grown to love Alabama and it was with reluctance that we moved back up north. And to make matters worse, we moved during my senior year of high school.

Woodism

*Even if you're running a fourth place race,
run as if you're in first.*

God Speed 89581

I graduated from North Central High School in December 1977, having given little thought as to what I wanted to do. Two months later, after Dad had fulfilled a one-year obligation in Indianapolis, he was offered an opportunity in Huntsville. A cemetery there wanted to start a mausoleum program, and because of Dad's previous success, they asked him to manage the project. Our family goal was always to return to Alabama, so we jumped at the chance, although not all of us made the move. Debbie was still in college in Columbus, and Lori, who had married, remained in Indianapolis. But Steve had recently returned from military service, and he did move with us.

After settling in Huntsville and working manual labor for almost a year, I decided a better option was to return to school. I applied to Vanderbilt University and was accepted. I planned to continue working and start the following semester. With his veteran status, Steve quickly gained employment at Redstone, home to several army commands and NASA's Marshall Space Flight Center, as an electrical/mechanical technician. He was hired to work on the initial testing phase of the new Space Shuttle Program at Martin Marietta, the prime contractor working on the Shuttle's External Tank. They were hiring additional technicians, and my brother put in a recommendation for me. With the potential for overtime and the temporary nature of the job, I thought this was the opportunity I was looking for as well as the resources I needed for school. I decided to go for it.

I was instructed to report to Building 4619 at Marshall Space Flight Center for a job interview with Martin Marietta. Because of my interest in history, I had done some research before my appointment. I learned that in 1941, during World War II, the State of Alabama had granted the federal government 160 acres of cotton fields to build an installation where an artillery plant could operate in relative obscurity. It got its name from the large amounts of ferric iron oxide that tinted the soil red. After the war, Dr. Wernher von Braun and a team of scientists launched a new field of "rocket science" at Redstone Arsenal. It was the precursor of a new federal agency, the National Aeronautics and Space Administration (NASA), in 1958. Shortly thereafter—in 1960—Marshall Space Flight Center (MSFC) was formed and took over a portion of the facility. It was named after General George C. Marshall, who facilitated what would be known as the Marshall Plan for the rebuilding of Europe after the war. Wernher von Braun was the first director of MSFC.

Marshall Space Flight Center Headquarters. Courtesy NASA

I was nineteen years old and in awe as I drove around searching for the correct building. By 1978, the sprawling Redstone Arsenal covered almost 40,000 acres, so it was not surprising that I took a couple of wrong turns, got lost, and arrived almost an hour late for my interview. I was stunned by the sheer size of the high bay area at Building 4619. I had never seen a structure of such magnitude—nearly 100 feet high and covering several acres. My interview was on the second level, in an office that overlooked the massive space-like structures below. Morley Robinson, a veteran employee from Martin Marietta headquarters in Denver, Colorado, was interviewing potential recruits for the new Space Shuttle Program. Fortunately, in spite of my being late, he invited me into his office. As I entered, he was chewing on a crusty cigar, and he continued to do so throughout the entire interview. It reminded me of a Bugs Bunny cartoon.

External Liquid Oxygen Tank (LOX)
Modal Test Stand. Courtesy NASA

I scanned the schematic drawings and artist renderings of the External Tank of the Space Shuttle that plastered the walls of his office. I was mesmerized by the size and scope of the project. Several pictures included people standing next to the tank, appearing ant-sized in comparison. My only exposure to the program had been from watching television when the orbiter Enterprise was carried atop a 747 and then released to test how it would land. I knew nothing about the External Tank or the Solid Rocket Boosters. The drawings were intriguing. I wanted to know more. I had a strong sense that this could be the opportunity I dreamed about as a young boy—an opportunity to participate in something that made a difference. I wanted the job. I knew that Steve had given me a great recommendation, but I was concerned that military veterans were getting preferential status in the selection process. I became even more unsettled when the interview lasted only ten minutes.

To my amazement, despite showing up late and having no related experience and only a high-school education, I was hired on the spot. The next day, October 20, 1978, I became known as Badge #89581. I was hired as a mechanical technician to perform a variety of tasks, including laying strain gauges, running electrical wires, building enclosures, and torquing bolts on the liquid oxygen portion of the External Tank located in the high bay. It didn't seem to matter to them that I knew nothing about strain gauges. In fact, I didn't even know what a strain gauge was. But I was willing to work twelve-hour days, seven days a week. I guess they figured I'd quickly learn or burn out trying.

On my first day on this new adventure, it would be an understatement to say that I was excited. My jaw dropped at the sight of the massive structures, and the jargon was a foreign language. The entire Space Shuttle Program seemed surreal. I had no idea what I was embarking on, but I knew it was something *big*.

My first official badge

It turned out that I was the last technician hired for the original testing crew as well as the youngest, which led to my "Mudman" predicament. According to safety regulations, I was assigned to a buddy system. Jack G. Harper—a.k.a. "Jack G"—another new hire and a seasoned Navy veteran, and I were practically joined at the hip. Jack G was ten years my senior and had the muscular structure of a football player. He was a heavy smoker and a hard drinker. We were both thrilled to be working on this new NASA program. He told me that he had done similar work in the Navy and promised to show me how to safety wire. I felt confident knowing I would learn what I needed to be successful.

Our initial task was to build a plastic enclosure around the center portion of the tank to ensure a temperature-controlled environment while technicians sprayed the tank with insulation foam. The tank was surrounded by metal wires connected to the tank with dental cement. To complete the enclosure, Jack G and I decided we had to cut one of the wires. During inspection of our work, we were asked, "Why the hell was the wire cut? It took us six damn months to calibrate the wires and now we'll have to reset them!" I looked to Jack G for guidance, and he stated rather matter-of-factly, "It was in the way of our enclosure." We were royally reamed out, to put it mildly, but that was how I learned about process instructions: Do not, and I mean *do not*, make any changes without all the correct paperwork! During the two weeks that we had to wait for recalibration, I learned that the wires were in place to measure the movement of the tank, and they had been carefully calibrated to measure data points. It was a learning process. Fortunately, that was not the last assignment for badge #89581 on the new Space Shuttle Program.

The testing phase of the Shuttle Program—and my work—on the External Tank was intended to last from six months to a year. In a short period, I developed a passion for the program, and I was eager to learn all I could about its capabilities and mission. I read everything I could get my hands on, asked questions, and gained an understanding of the bigger picture. This was going to be a huge program! I decided to put school on hold—at least through the testing phase. The plan was to build five orbiters with each to be launched 100 times, one every two weeks. (President Jimmy Carter later cut back the plan to four orbiters.) This ambitious schedule would require us to build twenty-four tanks per year. All tank assembly was to be performed at MSFC's Michoud Assembly Facility in New Orleans, Louisiana.

The External Tank (ET) was both the Shuttle's propellant tank and its structural backbone. The orbiter—whose tail-mounted three main engines drew their liquid oxygen (LO^2) and liquid hydrogen (LH^2) from the tank—is attached to the ET for flight. The ET is really two tanks in one: a forward liquid oxygen tank and a much larger liquid hydrogen tank at the rear. The two are connected by a relatively short corrugated cylinder called the intertank. In use, unlike the Solid Rocket Boosters (SRBs), which separate from the shuttle at 28 miles altitude, the ET stays attached to the orbiter for an additional six minutes, feeding it fuel and propelling it into orbit. It is jettisoned, empty, at the fringe of space. From there, it tumbles back to Earth, breaking up under controlled conditions as it reenters the Earth's atmosphere in a remote ocean area. It was the only major part of the Shuttle not reused, because recovery and reuse was not economically feasible. When NASA awarded the External Tank contract to Martin Marietta in 1973, they directed three test tanks to be manufactured. The first tank was the Main Propulsion Test Article (MPTA), which rolled out of the Michoud Assembly Facility on September 9, 1977. This was the first major milestone of the ET Project for the Space Shuttle Program. The MPTA held propellants for the 500+ seconds required to certify the cluster firing of all three main engines needed to launch the shuttle into orbit. This was a critical test program for certification performed at the National Space Technology Laboratory (NSTL) at Bay St. Louis, Mississippi. (It was later renamed Stennis Space Center after the late Senator John C. Stennis of Mississippi.)

First completed Space Shuttle External Tank
MPTA in 1977. Courtesy NASA

The second test tank was the Ground Vibrations Test Article (GVTA), which was tested at the Mated Ground Vibrations Test Tower in the East Test Area at MSFC in Huntsville, Alabama. This was the first time the shuttle was configured with all elements and was used for vibration testing purposes.

The third test tank was the Structural Test Article (STA) and consisted of two tanks—the liquid oxygen and liquid hydrogen tanks—and was located in separate areas at MSFC. Our team was initially assigned to perform stress analysis testing on the STA tanks.

This was an exciting time in the Space Shuttle Program, as we were beginning to see tangible evidence of progress, such as the GVTA tank, where we saw, for the first time, the orbiter, Enterprise, the External Tank, and the Solid Rocket Boosters mated together in a vertical flight configuration. This was a major milestone in the program. We were actually going to fly this amazing Wonder of the World!

Space Shuttle Orbiter, Enterprise, joined to GVTA tank and two SRBs in MSFC's Dynamics Test Stand. Courtesy NASA

My first white-knuckle experience was when I climbed fifty feet up the test stand to the nose forward end of the STA liquid oxygen tank to perform safety wiring. I was attached to the platform with a safety harness, and my equipment was tethered to my vest. It was exhilarating and nerve-wracking at the same time, so it took all I had to absorb what I was seeing and experiencing. After a couple light-headed episodes, I learned not to look down through the grillage. After the better part of a day, Jack G and I completed the installation of stainless-steel wires around the 92 bolts on the forward manhole of the tank to ensure that the bolts would not pop out during the fluid flow testing of the liquid oxygen tank. The installation and test were successful.

Modal Test Stand with STA Liquid Oxygen Tank. Courtesy NASA

While the liquid oxygen tank was being relocated for the next series—mud testing—I was in intensive hands-on training to become certified to lay and test strain gauges. This included blueprint reading, soldering, and tank entry in confined environments. I learned how to install strain gauges, and I would eventually install thousands of them. Each one was stamped with my badge number so it could be traced back to me for quality assurance purposes.

The tank was moved and suspended vertically from the high bay ceiling for the mud-testing series, and the baseline stress on the tank was calculated. Loading one million pounds of driller's mud into the tank would simulate the approximate weight of the oxygen while the Shuttle was thrusting and increasing in velocity, forcing the fuel downward against the aft portion of the tank.

But first, our team would enter the tank and lay strain gauges to measure the stresses on the tank loaded with the mud. Armed with schematic drawings and a tethered tackle box holding my supplies, I entered the tank for the first time. I vividly recall an overwhelmingly hypnotic feeling as I stood in the center of this enormous vessel. Everywhere I turned looked identical to where I had been, so I had to rely on the forward and aft manhole covers as my points of reference. I quickly acclimated to my new environment and spent the next several months laying strain gauges. The long hours were hardly glamorous, but the environment made every moment worth it.

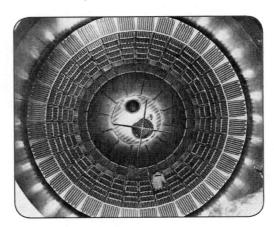

Liquid Oxygen Tank Interior. Courtesy NASA

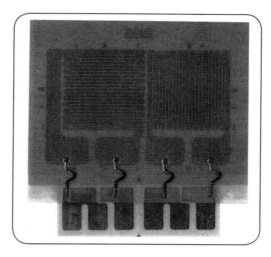

Strain Guage

After we installed, documented, calibrated, and tested more than 2,000 strain gauges, the tank was loaded with driller's mud for the stress testing. We ensured that it exceeded the analytical design models to determine any weakness in the seams or tank integrity. The testing was a success.

The final step was to drain the mud from the tank and clean the corrosive residue off the walls. A three-foot circular "Man Tube," which rotated 360 degrees from a thin cable system, was designed to lower one person, in a standing position, through the top of the forward manhole with a high-pressure water hose to spray the walls. The task was extremely dangerous, especially because of the confined space, and required a team member that had appropriate certification. I was chosen as the first person to test this device.

That was supposed to be the final major test of the STA liquid oxygen tank; however, our team was called in again to conduct a critical test that would replicate a problem that had occurred earlier on the GVTA tank that was attached to the orbiter Enterprise. An unexpected five- to ten-foot buckle in the forward ogive top section of the tank had occurred during testing while loading water in the unpressurized tank. (Water was used to simulate weight because the GVTA test stand was not supplied with a cryogenic storage capability for safety reasons.) A decision was made to conduct a test on the STA liquid oxygen tank with the same parameters to determine the reason for the GVTA buckle.

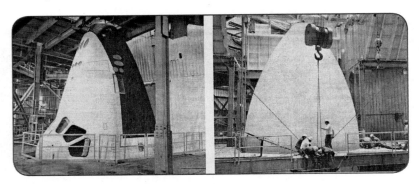

Enterprise Orbiter mated with GVTA Tank in
Dynamics Test Stand post-ET Buckle. Courtesy NASA

The STA liquid oxygen tank was carefully measured to ensure that it was of similar configuration. After we installed thousands of strain gauges, the tank was then de-pressurized. We were about 65 feet up on the test stand and about 100 feet away during the test. We heard a tremendous explosive sound due to the oscillation of the ogive panels—leading up to the buckle—which shook the test stand. It behaved exactly as the GVTA tank had and buckled almost identically in size and location, much like a crushed beer can. NASA photographers took pictures of the crushed tank. Everyone was evacuated from the test site because we were not sure what would happen when positive pressure was added to restore it to its approximate shape. If a hole had been created from the crushing energy, a tremendous amount of volume pressure could have escaped through a buckle hole and cause an explosion like what happens to an aerosol can.

Luckily, the tank held. Post assessment, it was concluded that the only way to remedy this anomaly was to maintain a minimum of 1.7 pounds per square inch pressure in the tank anytime propellant levels were greater than 2 percent. Because the fabrication of the first flight tank (ET-1) was well along and material already processed for six standard weight ETs, a decision was made to finish these tanks with the material on hand and put an operational constraint on the launch site to maintain the minimum pressure. If you ever see the STA tank on display, look up toward the nose and you will see the creases from the buckle in the ogive section of the tank.

Buckle on STA Tank. Courtesy NASA

Woodism

We all experience "mudman" moments. It's how we handle them that makes the difference.

Night Shift

B eing the new guy on the block, I was somewhat naïve about the ways my coworkers chose for having a little fun. In 1979, prior to the Shuttle flights, I had my first experience with a political "dog and pony show"—that is, "putting on the dog" to impress visitors. We were expecting a special guest: Congressman Ronnie Flippo, a member of the Science Committee in the House of Representatives and, therefore, a major influence on the NASA budget. It was important that Congressman Flippo and his entourage see us performing our work and be impressed with what he saw. Our team was instructed to have the facility in top-notch shape, to be visible while working, to maintain a safe environment, and to be on our best behavior. Well, three out of four isn't bad.

My coworkers, many of whom I fondly referred to as "Alabama rednecks," were aware that this was my first dog-and-pony show, but I was oblivious to the fact that I was the next guy in the box. We were performing stress analysis on the liquid hydrogen portion of the External Tank, installing strain gauges and soldering the wires. These tasks were labor intensive and required a high degree of concentration. We were conducting the work on a 300-foot test stand, and our only means of communication was via two-way radios.

Shortly before Congressman Flippo arrived, I was carefully installing a strain gauge, with tweezers, at the hundred-foot level. Just as I was about to place it on the tank, I asked my lead technician, "Scooter, how much do each of these strain gauges cost?" And just as he answered, "They're sixty dollars each," I glanced away and dropped the postage-stamp-sized gauge, never to be found again. My day went downhill from there.

A van pulled up carrying the congressman and the MSFC entourage, including NASA communications protocol personnel, the center director, and site management. I was meticulously performing my work and unaware that one of my coworkers was ten floors up, looking down through the grillage, grinning like a Cheshire cat, waiting for his moment to strike. The elevator carrying our visitors stopped at my work site as NASA management was explaining the process to Congressman Flippo and why he should vote additional monies for the program. At that moment, my coworker on the tenth floor turned on his two-way radio and yelled into my receiver—which was on full volume—"Beam me up, Scotty!" Members of the entourage looked at me as if I were an idiot and glanced up at the group on the tenth floor who were laughing hysterically. As the entourage left our area, I heard over the two-way radio, "Hey, Phillips. You've been initiated!"

Newbie on the Night Shift

The testing team consisted of a crew of twenty guys—ten on the day shift and ten on the night. I was assigned to the night shift. My supervisor, Bill Cunningham, was a former NASA employee on the Apollo Program and our overall operations lead. He was also a practical joker. I liked that about him. He once fashioned a black widow spider out of black tie wrap and waxed string used to bundle wires. He attached it to fishing line and suspended it over the door. He would drop it as select people came through the doorway. It went as planned until the NASA building manager came in and another team member decided to lower the spider and greet him face-to-face. He did not appreciate the joke. The sudden fright forced his head to snap backward, forcing his hard hat to fly off his head. We realized, at the point, the joke had gone too far. After a contrite apology and a promise to dismantle the practical joke, he replaced his hard hat and left shaking his head.

My team worked at a remote location on Redstone Arsenal known as the West Test Area, and we conducted most of our work on the West Test Stand. We were a diverse group of characters, but we learned to work well as a team, and we had each other's backs. Besides Steve and me, the team consisted of Mack Prozek, our lead engineer, who was an Air Force retiree. We feared him, knowing he was eyes and ears of our supervisor. W. B. Clifton, a.k.a. "Scooter," was the lead technician on the night shift and was well respected by the crew. We had several electrical/mechanical technicians, including Jack G. Harper, Dani Joe "DJ" Davis, Bob Stowell, Terry Craig (although the crew preferred to call him by his middle name, Monroe), David "Auggie Dog" Tipton, and Al Cupples, our foam technician, who was known as "Buzz" because of his predilection for weed. Like Steve, who always introduced me as his "baby" brother, they all treated me like a younger brother. I was happy to be on Steve's team once again. He took on a protective role initially, and I deferred to him. We looked similar so it was obvious that we were related. It became an ongoing joke that I was the cute one and he was the smart one. Only time would tell.

MSFC West Test Area. Courtesy NASA

I felt empowered by the enormous energy generated on the night shift. It was almost like a movie set when the bright lights lit up the test stand and the two perpetual ten-foot flames glowed like torches from the burn-off stack of the hydrogen storage facility a quarter-mile away. Security personnel kept vigil around the perimeter of the site to enforce authorized personnel access. There was always lots of hustle-bustle and continuous status announcements over the loud speakers. The familiar cool breeze and stunning night lights provided a pleasant backdrop. I was honored to be working on what I considered hallowed ground, knowing that Werhner Von Braun, President John F. Kennedy, and the futuristic visionary, Walt Disney, had likely stood in the very spot during the Saturn V program. These men had given inspiration and vision to a ten-year-old boy who dreamed of one day being part of something important, something that made a difference.

Werhner Von Braun with Walt Disney in MSFC
West Test area. Courtesy NASA

Werhner Von Braun with John F. Kennedy at MSFC.
Courtesy NASA

The team was preparing to embark upon a highly visible and potentially dangerous assignment: a first-time test of the Shuttle's STA liquid hydrogen tank, which had to be done prior to flight to certify that it could successfully hold the volatile hydrogen fuel at -423 degrees. There had already been a two-year delay in the program while NASA resolved a tile issue on the first orbiter, Columbia. The truth is that John Yardley, associate administrator at NASA headquarters, had made a bet that the External Tank, due to its complexity, would be the hold-up on the first Shuttle launch. As it turned out, the tile problem is what gave us the umbrella of time to perform the necessary testing to ready the tank for flight. Ultimately, anything less than total success would have meant another major delay.

We were using the same test stand that had been used for the Saturn V program, which certified the cluster firing of all five F1 engines from 1965-1967 and successfully put our first man on the moon. The test stand was in the West Test Area at MSFC and required a security badge to gain access due to the large quantities of volatile hydrogen fuel on site.

In transitioning the test stand from Saturn to the Shuttle, it was necessary to modify the 300-foot stand to accommodate the tank, which was 27.5 feet in diameter and 100 feet long with its inter tank attached. It was determined that weather elements, including wind from the open test stand, could possibly influence our critical series of tests, which included a force load interface test for the attach points of the two solid rocket boosters and the orbiter; the actual hydrogen load conditions in wet and dry environments; and a dry pressure test. To avoid compromising the results, Martin Marietta convinced NASA to install curtain-like windbreak sails at a cost of more than $200,000. The site preparation was complete. All systems were go.

STA Liquid Hydrogen Tank being removed from the
modified West Test Stand. Courtesy NASA

This is the first time this story is told. It was the largest test
to date by NASA on the Space Shuttle's External Tank program.
There were high-level "eyes" watching this particular test as it would
ultimately prove that we could, in fact, transition from Apollo/
Saturn to the Space Shuttle. One major screw-up would no doubt
halt the program indefinitely and obviously risk our personal
careers. It took some time to wrap my head around this event,
both the near-miss and the impact of what was accomplished.
This story will no doubt be controversial, but it is part of my story.
The following is my recollection of what happened.

Our assignment was to install a very complex and sophisticated
tool called a Liquid Hydrogen Tank Internal Access Platform,
which was designed by Martin Marietta at the Michoud Facility.
It provided access to the tank interior, thereby enabling the
installation, removal, replacement, and repair of equipment and
instrumentation. Personnel entry into the tank was made through
the aft manhole. Due to the complexity of this installation, just
one facet will be described, giving a view of the overall process.

Scott at Aft Liquid Hydrogen Manhole Cover

The tank was in a vertical flight-like configuration with a Class 1 tank environment. This means it had a controlled level of contamination and any incompatibility could result in an explosion when the hydrogen was loaded during testing. Our team was thoroughly trained and certified to perform tank entry in a confined environment, strain gauge installation, mating and de-mating connectors, and evacuation protocol similar to astronaut training. We were on the night shift, and it was a closed environment, meaning no media was present. The orbiter's tile issue dominated the press, and the tank held a minor interest at that point. As was customary for the night shift, we were developing procedures as we went along in order to maintain the highest level of safety. However, the truth is, it was a large task fraught with many unknowns, and it scared the crap out of us.

I entered the "clean room," which was positioned directly beneath the manhole, and donned my white "bunny" suit, clean cotton gloves, and non-skid Keds tennis shoes. I climbed up about seven feet on a wheeled safety ladder to enter through the

36-inch diameter manhole. From there, I hoisted myself into the tank and took position on the dome. Monroe was positioned at the forward bulkhead manhole 90 feet above and lowered a cable hook by an electrically powered winch. I carefully guided the hook down through the manhole to the waiting crew—Bob Stowell, Buzz, D. J., and Mack—who secured the access ladder and hoisted it back up through the manhole. I then positioned and secured the ladder that would provide us access to the major 2058 ring frame on the tank about ten feet up. The ring was a three-foot-wide ledge and provided us with 360-degree access around the inside perimeter of the tank to perform our tasks. The 2058 ring frame was also a load-bearing element and the critical location where the orbiter and solid rocket boosters were attached at the aft portion of the tank.

Interior Liquid Hydrogen dome with 2058 ring frame

The access platform consisted of hundreds of individual parts that had to be assembled piece-by-piece through the aft manhole. It was arduous and labor-intensive. It took two twelve-hour shifts of approximately eight team members to complete the task. Each piece had to be pulled out of its container, carried to the clean room, removed from the clean bag, wiped down with liquid freon, and the first piece fastened to the winch as it was lifted through the manhole. As each piece was added to the previous piece by ball-lock pins, Monroe carefully and slowly lifted it up through the tank until all the pieces were attached. I maintained my position on the ring frame and supervised as the platform pieces were raised.

The platform was now complete and dangling vertically in the center of the tank. Our next challenge was to bring this 28-foot, several thousand pound, very sophisticated platform into a horizontal position. This required two team members, Jack G and myself, on the ring frame pulling a tag line from the bottom toward us with all our strength. At the same time, Monroe simultaneously and gradually lowered the forward cable from above. We then cradled and latched the platform onto the ring frame creating a bridge over the dome. With the addition of further hardware and the motors, this would now allow us access to every square inch of the tank in order to install strain gauges and various instrumentation for the critical liquid hydrogen loading test series.

OPERATIONS AND MAINTENANCE MANUAL

SECTION XLVIII

TSE DATA SHEET

A78-3603   LH$_2$ INTERNAL ACCESS PLATFORM SET (VERTICAL)

December 11, 1978

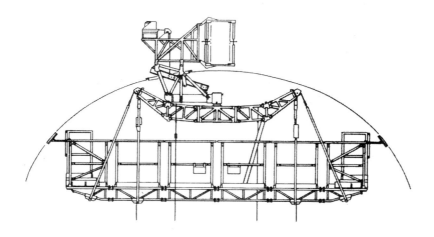

MARTIN MARIETTA AEROSPACE
Michoud Assembly Facility
New Orleans, Louisiana

Schematic of the internal access platform

MMC-ET-SE08c-4

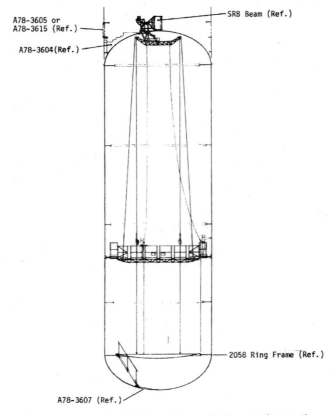

Figure 48-1. A78-3603 LH$_2$ Tank Internal Access Platform Set (Vertical).

48-2

Schematic of internal access platform installed in the hydrogen tank

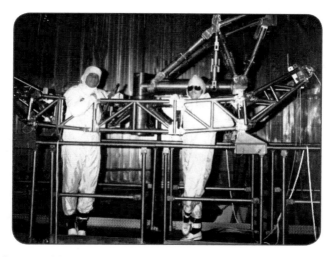

Scott and Steve on internal access platform. Courtesy NASA

When we returned to the next evening's shift to install the instrumentation sensors, we were very confident about the installation and NASA's quality acceptance of the platform. Standard procedures required that a tank monitor be stationed at the aft dome entry of the tank in the clean room beneath the manhole. This person was responsible for overseeing and documenting every detail of the work process, including keeping track of who entered and exited the tank. He was required to monitor and ensure a 21 percent oxygen flow within the tank—a critical assignment, as we preferred not to pass out while in the tank! He tethered and monitored all tools and equipment that entered the tank and accounted for the same tools and equipment as they were removed. He was also responsible for monitoring the electrical system that powered the equipment inside the tank, including the lifting platform and spotlights, and making sure that cables connected to the platform did not snag as we ascended and descended. We needed to stay in constant contact with the monitor, via radio, for status updates and external weather conditions because we were working in a potential lighting rod.

He was our lifeline, absolutely vital to our safety. Everyone was trained to be tank monitor, and the position changed nightly, selected at the beginning of the shift by drawing straws. On this particular night, Buzz drew the short straw.

It was our team's responsibility to install the strain gauges while traversing on the access platform. From the 2058 ring frame, Scooter and I stepped onto the motorized platform that was suspended by quarter-inch braided stainless-steel cables run by an electric motor called a sky climber, similar to a window-washer configuration. About one hour into our mission and halfway up the tank—approximately sixty feet high—our synchronized motors abruptly stopped. We radioed our tank monitor, "Hey, Buzz, we have no power. What is our status?" There was no response. Again, "Buzz, you down there?" We didn't know if he had passed out or what was going on.

We waited for the status over the radio, knowing that standard operating procedure was to manually descend in case of an emergency—something we didn't want to contemplate at that moment. Not only had the motors stopped, but we were in total darkness, suspended on our transport. The only light was coming through the manhole cover.

When we finally made contact with Buzz, he was unsure about the cause of the problem and hesitated a few moments. He then announced, "You're going to have to hand crank down."

Standard procedure if the motors shut down was to locate the emergency hand cranks embedded on either side of the motors, insert them on top, and manually crank the platform back down. The two of us manually moving several thousand pounds was an overwhelming process. The atmosphere quickly became very contentious, and we decided to take a short break before continuing the daunting task. During that time, Buzz realized that he had inadvertently kicked the plug and disconnected the power. He promptly replugged the cord, which immediately started the motors and activated the lights. Unfortunately, he failed to notify us prior to restoring the power. The cranks were still in place, and when the motor started, it threw both into the air. One handle flew past my face by about six inches and violently struck the sidewall of the tank.

We were stunned into total paralysis. I had been within inches of being knocked off the platform and into a fifty-foot fall, and the thought of a tank breach would have meant a potential catastrophic setback to an already tight program schedule. As quickly as we could regain our senses, which didn't seem very quickly, we proceeded to the bottom of the tank electrically. Fortunately, we had installed a parachute-type safety net to protect the dome in case anything should drop, and we located the handles, which had been absorbed into it. We then raised the platform to inspect where one of the handles hit. We found a slightly nicked area, which we determined had not been a breach of the tank wall. We carefully buffed out the scratch and marked the area for future inspection.

Upon exiting the tank, Scooter, the lead crew member, cussed Buzz out. As was often the case during the night shift, our safety guy was out of network range. The night supervisor, who was monitoring and overheard our dilemma, showed up to assess the situation. After much deliberation and a re-inspection of the site by the supervisor, it was determined that we should continue installing our instrumentation as scheduled. No incident report was filed, and we rewrote the procedures to circumvent a re-occurrence. Although we knew not to breathe a word about it, there had been a loud bang that evening, and for several weeks, we all sweat bullets for fear that someone outside of our team working that night might have decided to investigate the suspiciously strange noise.

It had been a case of Murphy's Law in action: If anything can go wrong, it will. Wouldn't you know that the only things not tethered—the hand cranks—were just the things we needed? As with the mudman incident, these hard lessons during the early testing phase needed to be learned so we could adjust the procedures and continue certification testing. It was because of our experience installing and uninstalling the access platform many times during the testing phase that we were able to expertly hone our skills. Over time, every piece of the access platform was as familiar to me as the back of my own hand. I even developed upgrades to improve the cable system. I received awards for developing a coiled wire system and lockable twist plugs so they couldn't be accidentally unplugged. Looking back, the challenging and dangerous lessons we learned during our early testing paved the way to successfully perform these same tasks on the first test tank and ultimately the maiden tank, ET-1.

George Jacobs (l), site manager, presenting awards to Scott, DJ Davis, and Bill Cunningham (r). Courtesy NASA

And now for the rest of the story. Buzz was reassigned, never to be tank monitor again. His new responsibilities included overseeing the disposition of leftover components—known as Part A and Part B—that formulated the insulation foam. Surplus liquid foam components had to be poured back into their original containers to avoid causing a chemical reaction. One day, after a "liquid lunch," he came back to clean the machine that mixed the foam. Inadvertently, he poured 10 gallons of Part A into a 55-gallon drum of Part B, tightened the bung cap, and walked away. Within minutes, the bung popped and the 55-gallon drum exploded, immediately filling the room with foam. Everything in the room was destroyed. We never saw Buzz again after that incident.

Weeks later, we were in the middle of uninstalling the access platform from the tank. Monroe, our team member in charge of setting up the electrical details that night, left for his lunch break. When he returned, after passing through the security gate, he appeared to be in high spirits. Just as he radioed down to check on our status, we saw a scantily dressed blonde peering down into the tank at us. We recognized her as one of the go-go dancers from a local nightclub. He apparently told her about his work, and she convinced him to let her see up-close. When we asked how he was able to get her through security, he said, "I smuggled her on site in my trunk."

There was never a dull moment on the night shift!

Woodism

*Prepare the best you can, but
expect the unexpected.*

ET-1

One night, our new tank monitor, Jerry Cross, mentioned that his cousin had an old guitar for sale. He thought it was a Martin. Knowing that I played, he asked if I might be interested. C. F. Martin is the oldest guitar company in the country, and I considered their guitars to be the finest made. So yes, I was interested.

A couple weeks later, during an extended lunch break on the night shift, Jerry and I took a thirty-minute drive north to the hills of Tennessee. I could never have retraced our route through all the twists and turns and dirt back roads. We finally rumbled up a gravel road to a one-room house. As we approached the porch, we heard voices inside and realized a card game was going on. We knocked and his cousin invited us in. Inside the smoke-filled room, a group of about six pistol-packing, redneck hillbillies were drinking beer and playing Rook. A topless woman was breast-feeding an infant in the middle of it all.

Jerry told his cousin that I was the guy interested in the guitar. He led us behind a curtain to what served as the bedroom. From under the bed, he pulled out a hard-shell Gibson case covered with dust and cobwebs. He unlatched the case, revealing a small body guitar without strings. I saw the C. F. Martin logo on the back of the headstock and recognized it to be an authentic vintage model. It looked to be in average condition, and I offered what I had in my pocket—$150 cash—for the case and all. My offer was accepted and I headed home with my treasure.

I later checked the serial number, and an inquiry to C. F. Martin confirmed that the guitar, Model #1-17, Serial #49206, was built in 1931. I put on new strings and have been playing it ever since. This fueled a lifelong interest in the C. F. Martin Co., a legacy that dated to 1833. Plus, the company's system of authentication later inspired me to add serial numbers to my own artwork and to secure meticulous documentation of my journey through the Space Shuttle Program, thereby creating my own legacy.

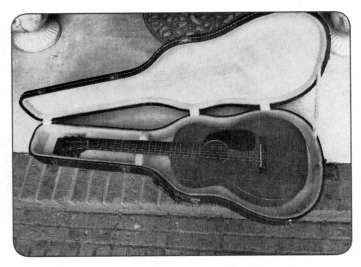

Vintage C. F. Martin guitar, Model #1-17

The guitar sparked my curiosity in another way and became part of an experiment. The STA tank, due to its vastness and cylindrical design, created unique sound reverberations. Communicating with team members across the tank was next to impossible until we figured out that the way to avoid the reverb was to speak normally toward the wall of the tank and the sound would travel around to the other side clear as a bell. With that in mind, I was eager to hear how music would echo in the tank. I'd lie on the parachute safety net during lunch and strum my guitar. The acoustics inside the tank sounded amazingly soft and quite professional. I learned something else: People can listen to "Take Me Home, Country Roads" just so many times during a single lunch break. The words "Shut the hell up, Phillips!" were my first clue to this response mechanism.

In 1980, one year out from the maiden Shuttle launch and due to our success on the early test program at MSFC, our team was selected to perform major modifications on the aging MPTA test tank at National Space Technology Laboratory (NSTL) in Bay St. Louis, Mississippi. As NASA's largest rocket engine testing facility, NSTL is where the three main engines were being certified flight ready. The tank had been cycled many times with cryogenic fuels to certify the three main engines, and our team was tasked with installing the access platform to replace the worn-out instrumentation.

Test Stand Access Badge

Three main engines installed on Orbiter MPTA
boattail in the Test Stand at NSTL

The Space Shuttle Program was one of the largest, most sophisticated undertakings ever attempted, and my work and that of my coworkers had enormous implications for the future of our country. I had been working with an impressive group of people for three years, but it was during our temporary duty (TDY) at NSTL that we became a well-oiled, highly functioning "team." Our core team consisted of Scooter as the lead, Steve contributed electrical expertise, and Jack G, DJ, and I made the work happen. What a ride it was! From the depths of the tank to the heights of the test stands, I found my work exhilarating. I was often overcome with the pride that I knew our country would feel when we launched the first Shuttle into space.

Test Team (l. to r.) Steve, Scott, DJ, Scooter, and Jack G

One evening, while standing on the tenth floor of the 407-foot NSTL B-1/B-2 test stand, I was overlooking the buffer zone to the Mississippi test range in the middle of the Bayou Swamp, which was swarming with alligators. There was a cool breeze across my face, and I just had to stop and process all that I was fortunate to experience. It was the end of my shift, and I was on my way down to an awaiting Thunderbird and off to close the evening with a couple beers and talk of the Shuttle program at a local bar with our new found friends.

During the many months of TDY at NSTL, my team continued its heavy work schedule. When we got a break, we looked for a little fun, and New Orleans—fifty miles west of Bay St. Louis—was certainly a good place for doing that. Two of our favorite spots were on Bourbon Street and in the suburb Fat City. I spent my twenty-first birthday at Mardi Gras, catching so many beads from topless women that it took me an hour to remove them all from around my neck. Mardi Gras was the biggest party in the world, and we made it a point to be there from then on.

On my third trip to Mardi Gras, I was invited to a formal ball by my colleague, Mike McCann, who was a member of the Mardi Gras Baucus Krewe—a group that had sponsored a float for the last 100 years. After completing the final parade, the 100-foot Bauci Gator float rolled into the convention center for its grand finale. I had donned a rented tuxedo and was waiting in line with Edwin Edwards, the governor of Louisiana, to enter the coveted event. I proceeded to my designated table and recognized the actor Ed Nelson, who sat down next to me. I introduced myself and said, "I have to confess, my parents made me go to bed when *Peyton Place* came on the television." We had a good laugh and the evening got better by the minute. During the meal, I looked around the room and saw many familiar faces, such as Dutch Morial, mayor of New Orleans, actors Steve Guttenberg (*Diner* and *Cocoon*) and Ron Glass (from TV's *Barney Miller*), many famous jazz musicians including clarinetist Pete Fountain and singer Michael Bolton, to name a few. Lively conversation and abundant wine flowed long into the night. I decided that was the best way to experience Mardi Gras!

Scott and Mike McCann at Mardi Gras Ball

One night Steve, Scooter, DJ, Jack G, and I stopped in at Spinnakers in Fat City. It happened to be "Schnapps Night," and it didn't take long for Jack G to get tanked. His wife had joined us, and when someone in the bar accidentally bumped into her, he decided it was time to hit heads. At a little over 6 feet tall and 225 pounds, he easily picked up our table and threw it on the dance floor. As he moved toward the culprit, several of us jumped him in an attempt to hold him back. We somehow managed to get him out to the parking lot, but he had the car keys. He was adamant about driving, and the only thing that saved us was when he passed out. I never developed a taste for Schnapps, so I became the designated driver. Halfway back to our hotel, DJ, who was seated in the passenger's seat and always watched my back, remarked, "Whoa, man, the car sounds funny." I was so rattled by the experience that I didn't realize I had been driving in second gear the whole way.

A few months later, after a twelve-hour shift, Steve, Scooter, Jack G, and I decided to visit the gentleman's club we liked to frequent. We were having a few drinks and minding our own business when a man landed on our table with his throat cut from ear to ear. Our drinks flew in the air as the table collapsed, sending us out of our chairs in disbelief. The lights quickly came on and the police arrived in what seemed like mere seconds. They promptly handcuffed a guy at the bar. As Jack G was picking up the table, Scooter yelled, "Let's get the hell out of here!" As we picked up our belongings from the floor, Steve grumbled, "Damn! I have blood on my jacket!" On the way out, I noticed the dancers continued to perform throughout the entire ordeal. I could only assume it wasn't the first time they had witnessed such a scene. For me, it was to be my last time. I chose to stay away from New Orleans barrooms from then on.

After the successful completion of modifications on the MPTA tank, our team returned to Huntsville in mid-1980. The test program was winding down, and I had the crushing realization that I might not be able to continue on through the operational phase of the Shuttle program. My original commitment had been for only the testing program, and now that I could see the big picture, I knew there was so much more.

Successful cluster firing of Shuttle's three main engines

When we were all directed to attend a mandatory meeting, I figured the handwriting was on the wall. The meeting was led by a representative from New Orleans who came to Huntsville to issue directives for the new lightweight tank post-ET-1, a phase that would require fewer workers. It was rumored that we would have to drop 10 percent of our workforce, which meant one person. I had been forewarned, off the record, by my supervisor, Bill Cunningham, that because I was the last guy hired, I was most likely going to be the first person laid off. So there I sat, contemplating what my future would look like without the Shuttle.

A team member on the day shift, David Tipton, was also at the meeting. "Auggie Dog," as we called him, had been with the company about a year longer than I had, and we knew him to be very temperamental—and that is an understatement. One of my recollections of him was when he lost change in a soda machine. It made him so angry that he tipped over the machine and jumped on it with all of the might in his 6-foot 3-inch frame. As the meeting began and it was announced that one individual would be let go from the program, Auggie Dog stood up and said, "Well, don't that just suck!" It was soon disclosed that he was the one being let go. That was the moment that propelled me onto the operations phase of the program and provided the opportunity for a thirty-year career. Fate or happenstance?

Dodging that bullet was a turning point for me, and my career moved to a new phase. The original night shift team— Steve, Scooter, Jack G, DJ, and myself, with the addition of Mack Prozek as supervisor and Jim Turner as quality—were selected to go to the Kennedy Space Center (KSC) in August 1980 to work on the ET-1 maiden flight vehicle. Our task was to repair and/ or replace damaged sensors and wiring inside the ET-1. This was a highly visible and demanding position. The eyes of the nation would be on us. It was our Super Bowl moment.

ET-1 Maiden Flight Vehicle delivered to KSC. Courtesy NASA

Steve and I prepared the access platform kit and shipped it to the Vehicle Assembly Building (VAB) at KSC to be installed in the ET-1 tank. On our arrival at KSC, our team updated certifications for astronaut-level training, including height hazards, hypergolic fuels, solid propellants, emergency escape procedures, and confined environment training prior to working in the VAB.

As a boy, I had dreamed of what it must have been like to be the first man on the moon, and here I was working in the very building that was used to put Neil Armstrong there during the Apollo/Saturn program.

We entered the VAB and made the necessary preparations to work on the unmated ET-1 in highbay #4. Prior to donning our clean-room suits with hoods, gloves, and tethers, we drew straws to see who would be the designated tank monitor. I prayed I wouldn't draw the short straw, as I really wanted to be part of the inside team. Luckily, I made it on the inside.

We removed the 92 bolts on the manhole cover and purged positive pressure inside the tank. It was the first time the tank had been opened since making the 900-mile journey on the barge from New Orleans. We waited for clearance when the tank had reached a level of 21 percent oxygen, the level necessary to keep us from passing out while inside.

When we entered ET-1, which was in a vertical position, it was pitch black and rather eerie, like a crypt. The air felt dry and an echo reverberated off the walls, reminding us of how vast it was. We switched on our high-beam flashlights and immediately noticed the inside of the tank was a brilliant glistening yellow from the iridite, an anti-corrosive chemical used only on flight vehicles to ensure a super-clean tank. We worked the day shift, which was unusual for our team. We weren't used to having an abundance of NASA safety and quality people buzzing around, and it actually made us a little nervous.

Inside flight-ready ET-1. Courtesy NASA

We worked one twelve-hour shift to install the internal access platform in ET-1, allowing us entry to the LH2 forward bulkhead where the sensors were located. Even though each piece had to be craned up 100 feet just to reach the tank, our team had so fine-tuned the installation that we finished well within schedule. The only snafu that day was when a NASA photographer documenting the process dropped his lens cap into the dome of the tank. As with the hand cranks, the lens cap was successfully retrieved from the safety net that was installed to protect the dome.

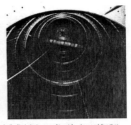

External tank operations employees work on modifications inside the liquid hydrogen tank at Kennedy Space Center. In the first photo, one of two tripod assemblies that help stabilize the two-person movable platform during assembly and dismantling is installed. Tag lines leading to a swiveling beam assembly are checked in the center photo. In the photo at right, the platform is raised inside the 97-foot long liquid hydrogen tank. The platform, attached to a swiveling beam assembly, can rotate 360 degrees to permit access to the total length of the tank.

(series of three pictures) Our Team installing the Access Platform inside ET-1 at KSC. Courtesy NASA

Steve and I were selected, along with a NASA quality control representative, to proceed onto the lift platform to replace the 100 percent liquid hydrogen engine cutoff level sensor, which was 90 feet up. With our tethered handles embedded in the motors, we traversed to the top. Upon inspection, we found nicked wires and an identification tag adhering to the liquid hydrogen mast that should have been removed by the manufacturer. Because this was a Type 1 tank, this held the potential for causing an explosion during flight. Just one undiscovered defect like that could affect many lives—astronauts, their families, and all of the Shuttle workers. The efforts of thousands could be permanently erased by such a seemingly tiny detail. We sealed the wires, replaced and confirmed the eco sensor, and removed the tag.

Liquid Hydrogen Level Sensor Mast that was
removed and repaired. Courtesy NASA

We waited about two weeks for final testing of the level sensors and then reentered the tank to remove the access platform piece-by-piece. The tank was now flight ready. Prior to sealing the manhole cover, the NASA quality inspector verified that everything had been removed. Our final tasks were to remove the ladder, wipe down the dome with liquid Freon, and detach the "Remove Before Flight" ribbon. As we dropped out of the tank, with me as the last person out, the quality inspector pulled the ribbon (Serial #000306) off the dome area and passed it to me to celebrate my journey and mark me as the last person out of the ET-1 tank. Standard operating procedure is to cut the ribbon in half and place it in the quality book. Instead, we made a copy of the ribbon, and I kept the original. Our team received a "Zero Latent Defect" award for our successful work on ET-1.

Original Remove Before Flight Ribbon

With our work inside the tank finished, we returned to Huntsville, confident that everything was a go for launch. However, NASA engineers raised concerns that ice could form on the tank when it was loaded with its super-cold fuel, which might dislodge at liftoff and damage the orbiter's protective tiles. Martin Marietta quickly mobilized its foam operations to KSC to resolve one of the most difficult modifications required to the tank. To prevent ice from forming on critical areas of the tank exterior, molded pieces and additional foam insulation were strategically added to the orbiter side of the tank.

In November 1980, the tank was moved from the highbay holding area to the mobile launcher platform across the aisle into an adjoining cell and mated with the SRBs as a "stack." Because of a tight clearance, the tank was attached to a special three-legged sling—hooked to a 250-ton crane—designed to keep the tank perfectly vertical during the move. The tank was hoisted to a height permitting clearance and lowered to its flight position between the two solid rocket boosters. The tank was precisely aligned for the descent to capture the booster's guide pins. This was a historical milestone as the two flight vehicles managed at MSFC were mated together for the first time. The orbiter, Columbia, soon completed the full stack configuration.

Orbiter Columbia ready to mate with ET-1 and SRBs. Courtesy NASA

By mid-December, the Shuttle began a series of flight-readiness testing. The firing test included loading the hydrogen, a full launch countdown, and firing of the three main engines for twenty seconds—a full up demonstration of the propulsion system. This was critical to prove the system was viable. The second test, on the Shuttle interface, included a full stack verification of electrical systems and, for the first time, astronauts Bob Crippen and John Young simulating the orbiter systems. Unlike Apollo, this vehicle would be test flown by these two men for the first time. John Young was a veteran astronaut and the ninth man on the moon as commander of Apollo 16. Bob Crippen had never flown. He was a rookie astronaut. I can only imagine what was going through their minds as they went through the final flight tests, knowing that their moment was approaching and their lives would be on the line as the Shuttle flew, for the first time, in its full configuration.

All systems responded appropriately with minor electrical instrumentation and valve issues in the SRBs and a replacement part on the three main engines. No changes were required on the External Tank. The successful flight readiness tests paved the way for the Shuttle to move to launch pad #39A in January 1981 in preparation for a March launch.

While on the launch pad, validation tests were conducted to verify connections between the launch pad platform and ground systems. The External Tank was filled with 383,000 gallons of -423 degrees hydrogen fuel and then drained to verify it would hold. A couple days later, the tank was loaded with 143,000 gallons of -297 degree liquid oxygen and then drained. Two separate fueling tests were conducted to circumvent a potential explosion should one tank fail. Technicians checked for ice or instrumentation issues during the cryogenics loading and unloading.

During the post inspection, it was discovered that two large areas of foam—7- by 8-feet and 4- by 4-feet—on the orbiter side of the tank had debonded. Our team quickly mobilized to resolve the problem. We were dispatched to strip the foam from the MPTA test tank in NSTL in Bay St. Louis, Mississippi, and refine the process of applying the primer and foam. We worked around the clock to resolve the issue. It was a complex process because the tank shrinks during the loading of cold fuels and expands when drained. We refined the bare aluminum cleaning process using demineralized water, meticulously heated the area both inside and outside the tank to a curing temperature, applied an exact thickness of primer, allowed the primer to cure, and manually applied the foam. NASA decided not to hold up the flight readiness firing of the three main engines while we came up with the foam fix. So while we were resolving the foam issue, NASA prepared for the firing test.

In February, the wet countdown demonstration was conducted. This included a first-time loading of both fuels, a fifty-three-hour countdown, and a twenty-second firing of the three main engines. To prevent any foam from falling off during the loading of fuel and subsequent engine firing, a cargo net with straps was temporarily wrapped around the tank during testing. The test was successful and put us a major step closer to the maiden flight. Due to the foam issue, the new launch date was moved to April 5.

Cargo net positioned around the tank to hold foam. Courtesy NASA

Back in NSTL, we stripped the tank, reapplied the foam, loaded the fuels, and performed testing. Our test methods on the MPTA test tank were successful and we were given the green light on March 4. The foam team moved their operation to KSC to make the repairs to ET-1—and successfully completed their work in record time and ready for the April launch. There would not be another "wet" loading of fuel on the pad, and NASA went on faith that the foam fix would work. We were confident but remained on pins and needles.

The successful flight readiness firing and repair of the foam prepared the Shuttle for the final "dry" countdown test on March 23. This was a thirty-three-hour dress rehearsal for the flight and launch crew. Bob Crippen and John Young entered the orbiter at the two-hour mark of the countdown for the final system checks. Everything went smoothly until late in the countdown when there was a ten-minute delay because of a mechanical discrepancy between the ground and flight computers, which was quickly resolved.

Astronauts Bob Crippen, pilot, and John Young, Commander. Courtesy NASA

The successful testing was marred by a tragic event that occurred about an hour after the test was completed. Five technicians were cleared by NASA safety supervisors to enter a rear section of the orbiter above the engine during a purge of the orbiter, a routine procedure that used nitrogen to flush all the oxygen out of the engine compartment prior to test-firing. All five of the men were asphyxiated by the odorless, colorless gas; they lost consciousness before anyone realized anything was amiss. Two of them died. A sixth technician discovered them and alerted a security guard who donned an air pack and dragged the victims from the compartment. Following a three-month investigation, it was concluded that a last-minute change in testing procedures and a miscommunication caused the accident. This horrific loss of life triggered an immediate stand-down until all personnel with access to confined environments were recertified. Our motto on the night shift was always safety first, but this was a stark reminder to us of the importance of maintaining 21 percent oxygen in a confined environment and of how potentially dangerous and complex our work was.

After we resolved the foam issue in New Orleans for ET-1, our team returned to Huntsville. We were anticipating the first launch, which was scheduled in a few months, and we had begun work on the new lightweight tank program at MSFC. NASA had tasked us with reducing the heavy version of the tank, 6,000 pounds, in preparation for STS-6.

Normally, I would be working into the evening, but on the eve of the 1980 presidential election, a test was being conducted on the tank, and so I had the night off. A NASA colleague, Joe Jackson, who was associated with the Democratic party, invited me to help set up chairs at the airport for a last-minute campaign speech by First Lady Rosalynn Carter as she made a brief stop at the airport in Huntsville. He assured me there would be plenty of food. I knew it was going to be very cold that night, but being a single guy, I was never one to turn down free food. I also thought it would be a memorable experience to see a sitting First Lady, so I agreed to go.

We parked our cars at the airport parking and approached the roped-off tarmac where Secret Service agents were handing out badges. There was only one way in and one way out as people lined up to get into the event. The Secret Service staff patted down everyone inside the ropes and pinned on their access badges. With Joe's credentials, we were ushered past the crowds. As we approached the front of the line, they ran out of visitor badges, and the only ones left were for VIPs. They pinned a VIP badge on my red ski vest and cleared me through, with strict instructions to return the badge when we were finished setting up the chairs.

About thirty minutes later, a small aircraft landed on the airstrip. As the doors opened, one of the Secret Service agents motioned for us to help with the suitcases. We were surprised to see Tom T. Hall, the country music singer, standing with his guitar case and luggage, which were plastered with bumper stickers that said "Another Farmer for Carter." We talked for a moment about guitars. I told him about my vintage 1931 Martin and he told me that his guitar formerly belonged to Johnny Rodriguez, the first Latin American country music singer. He went on to the event, and we were instructed to take his belongings to the airport hotel where he was staying. On arriving in his hotel room, I saw an amazing amount of liquor bottles set up in anticipation of his arrival. All I could think of was that that was going to be one hell of a party! As I was leaving the room, the perpetual collector in me decided to test one of the stickers on his guitar case. I easily peeled off one of the "Another Farmer for Carter" bumper stickers as a memento and placed it inside my vest to avoid detection.

Back at the airport tarmac, the chairs were neatly in place and the Secret Service table had been removed. Because I was still wearing the VIP badge, I was cleared back onto the tarmac. As I was sitting there freezing, waiting for Rosalynn Carter to arrive, I was glad that I had worn my ski vest, and I reflected on how easy it had been for me to move through security.

As the First Lady's plane landed, I was surprised when the Secret Service asked me, along with several others, to move the gantry. I found myself at the foot of the steps as Mrs. Carter began her descent. I had completely forgotten that I was wearing a VIP badge. As she walked down the stairs toward me, she made eye contact and motioned for me to take her arm. I escorted her to the stage about a hundred feet away. As she was being introduced and the crowd cheered from behind the ropes, I walked her to the foot of the steps. I noticed a gentleman in the crowd with a Polaroid camera and motioned for the man to take my picture with Mrs. Carter to document the event. He snapped a picture and tossed it my way. I put it in my vest pocket for safekeeping—and to provide the warmth for it to develop properly. As Mrs. Carter started toward the podium, she turned and gave me a gentle kiss on the cheek and a very gracious "thank you." As the night wore on, my serendipitous experience felt more and more unreal.

I later shared the events with my family. Faced with a little disbelief on their parts, I suddenly remembered the Polaroid shot, but as it turned out, the man who took the picture failed to capture our heads! The next day at work, I told my coworkers I had escorted the First Lady of the United States during her visit to Huntsville. They looked at me as if I had just come off of a major drunk. But the stars must have been lined up on that cold November night! A local reporter covering the story saw my name tag next to the VIP badge and mentioned in his article that I was the main security man and had escorted First Lady Rosalynn Carter to the stage.

Campaign Stop Memorabilia

Scooter and I drove to Kennedy Space Center to witness the maiden flight of the Space Transportation System (STS-1). It was scheduled to launch April 10, 1981, but because of a computer inconsistency indicating that the redundancy system was not communicating with the onboard system, the date had to be scrubbed and rescheduled to April 12.

Because this was the first manned test flight, the implications—and risks—were huge. While awaiting the next window of opportunity, I thought about astronauts Bob Crippen and John Young, who were bravely anticipating their flight on STS-1. They are true American heroes. I also contemplated all of the firsts we would achieve: the first launch of a recoverable and reusable manned spacecraft, the largest solid rockets ever to be flown, the first time men would fly on solid rockets, the highest-performance rocket engine in history, the largest liquid hydrogen engine ever developed or flown, the first launch of a rocket system manned on its maiden flight, and the first recovery of a primary propulsion system intact. The implications were overwhelming as well as our national pride and prestige.

STS-1 prior to launch.

There were millions of components and myriad situations that could have occurred. But still, on April 12, 1981, STS-1 successfully launched into space. The moment is forever fixed in my mind. It was extremely emotional for me. It's difficult to describe that feeling, standing alongside a half-million eager spectators, less than three miles away from Pad #39A, waiting for the first Shuttle launch, and knowing I played a part in it. The countdown by the launch team and the telemetry information over the loudspeaker was surreal. Then there were the cheers and excitement as all eyes fixed at the brilliant yellow glow of the SRBs igniting. I heard the familiar rumbling of the engines and the crescendo of SRBs and engines firing—for the first time—together. I had my camera ready but at the last instant chose to experience the sights and the sounds through my eyes rather than a lens. The Shuttle ascended into space with an unexpected popping sound, and I followed the corkscrew contrail until it disappeared. I wiped tears of joy that trickled down my cheeks. I was filled with pride and humbled at the same time. It was a life-altering experience. This was the beginning of an important contribution to the future of our country.

Launch of STS-1 on April 12, 1981. Courtesy NASA

STS-1 Flight Patch

During our drive home to Huntsville, I had an epiphany of sorts. I felt that something had been ignited in me. The Shuttle was the vehicle for my childhood dream and a way to express my creativity and be part of something larger than myself. I was inspired to document the program through collecting memorabilia and by recording my firsthand experiences. I began to amass anything related to the Shuttle, including astronaut signatures. My coworkers would laugh and say, "If there are astronauts around, you'll see Phillips."

It was around this time that my nickname became "Shuttleman," and I would soon realize a way to turn my love for woodworking into Shuttle art. I embarked on a quest that would continue throughout the entire program and beyond.

Woodism

Strive to be part of something larger than yourself.

Family Business

B ack on the home front, my dad had finally come to terms with his ambition of becoming an entrepreneur. My parents were excited about starting a bulk-mail processing facility in Huntsville, the only one in North Alabama. Because I had always been the hands-on guy in the family, they urged me to step up and help them get their business off the ground. Knowing the time commitment I would be making, I wondered, "Do I turn right or left?" Our family had always pulled together during challenging times, especially during the years my parents had their Amway business, and this was another opportunity for them to achieve their dream. Besides, I could still work on the Space Shuttle Program. It wouldn't take that much time. Would it?

It's amazing how one year turns into another and another. For the next ten years, after finishing my day at Martin Marietta, I would drive to my parent's facility to begin an evening of processing bulk mail, loading and unloading materials, and repairing equipment. There was always a tight schedule, and I often worked well past midnight.

I had little social life, but I continued to indulge my passion for tinkering and woodworking. One of the benefits of working the family business was being able to use available space in the warehouse. I set up a small shop in the back of the business and retreated to my "unheated man cave" at every free moment. For the first time, I was able to organize my tools, equipment, and materials. With everything easily at hand, I felt more energized and productive. I stayed motivated throughout the mind-numbing hours of running mail machines by thinking of creative projects I could build in my workshop, and I looked forward to unwinding after a long day.

I designed and crafted my first Shuttle model. Then another and another. Initially, I gave my models away, as I felt guilty charging for my crude representations. But I was enjoying the process. After my coworkers learned of my hobby, I also began to develop a repertoire of professional awards and plaques I could produce—more reasons to spend time in my workshop.

First Shuttle Model

I gradually came to appreciate my rich inner life. I was empowered. My enthusiasm for woodworking, space history, and space memorabilia increased dramatically, almost exponentially, at times. In the beginning, I couldn't comprehend why other people weren't as passionate as I was. Although I learned not to take it personally if others didn't "get" my interests. The truly exciting moments are always when I share my passions and sense a spark igniting in someone else.

As the mail business cycled through political election seasons, we found candidate mailings to be very lucrative. Every other year, we counted on processing mail pieces for local and state politicians running for office. One evening in 1982, we prepared a flyer for a George C. Wallace rally in Huntsville during his campaign for his fourth term as governor of Alabama. I was aware of Wallace's controversial civil rights record and how it almost collided with the future of our space program in Huntsville.

After President Kennedy acknowledged his goal of landing a man on the moon, on several occasions, he visited Wernher von Braun and his team of rocket scientists at Redstone Arsenal, where the propulsion system was being developed for the Saturn V program. On May 12, 1963, the nation watched on TV as Birmingham Police Commissioner Eugene "Bull" Connor shamefully sprayed water hoses and unleashed attack dogs on protesters seeking desegregation and economic opportunities for blacks. The president delivered a speech condemning the racial strife and ordered federal troops nearby as a show of disapproval of the state's actions. Wallace publicly called President Kennedy a military dictator for challenging states' rights.

One week later, on May 18, Kennedy began his three-stop visit to the South in Nashville, Tennessee. From there, he helicoptered to Muscle Shoals, Alabama, to commemorate the thirtieth anniversary of the Tennessee Valley Authority. It was there he met up with Gov. Wallace, prior to their meeting at Redstone Arsenal. During the fifteen-minute helicopter ride to Huntsville, Kennedy reminded Wallace that the federal government controlled the purse strings for the space program. Wallace assured the president that he would handle the unrest. A mere three weeks later, on June 11, Governor Wallace stood in the doorway of the University of Alabama, denying access to blacks at the school. After that incident, Wallace continued to disagree with Martin Luther King Jr. on civil rights and the federal government interfering with states' rights, but stepped back from his aggressive actions and conceded to a federal court order allowing racial integration. That was the final encounter between Wallace and Kennedy; President Kennedy was tragically assassinated five months later on November 22, 1963.

President Kennedy's final visit to Alabama (l to r) Governor George Wallace, Alabama Senator John Sparkman, President John F. Kennedy, and Congressman Bob Jones. Courtesy NASA

I was intrigued by how contrasting political personalities—along with the complexities of their views—could find common ground, albeit sometimes through coercion, to accomplish incredible goals. Despite Wallace's arrogant and misguided actions, Alabama's strong congressional team, headed by Senator John Sparkman and Congressman Bob Jones, was able to hold the space program together in Huntsville.

I decided to attend the Wallace rally advertised on the flyer. I was curious to experience this complex and controversial man up close. A person who so blatantly perpetuated social unjust and could have single-handedly brought down the future of our space program in Huntsville. Upon arriving at the event, I ran into my supervisor, Bill Cunningham, who was a lieutenant in the Alabama National Guard. He was there as a rally volunteer and invited me to help park cars. He added, "I have backstage passes to personally meet Governor Wallace, and you can meet him too." Yes, I was definitely interested.

As people arrived, I recognized numerous local politicians whom we had done mailings for, as well as George Wallace Jr., the governor's only son, who drove up in a white Thunderbird. After we finished our work, we entered the building and stood in the back. The convention hall wasn't air conditioned and it was sweltering hot. I heard Wallace yell, "If it's too hot in the kitchen, get the hell out!" There were rally signs everywhere with the same sentiment.

After a loud and rousing thirty-minute rally, the energized, raucous crowd was on their feet. It was almost a carnival scene with local politicians and people from all walks of life. People were smoking and chewing tobacco and hoisting signs and banners. They were both cheering and challenging Wallace, "Tell it like it is! Keep the federal government out of our business!" Several people passed out after being overcome from the heat, leading to screams of, "Get that lady some water. She's passed out!" A line began to form to shake the governor's hand. Bill and I happened to be at the front of the line. As I waited my turn to meet the governor, thoughts ran through my mind of his past civil rights views and how he almost collided with Kennedy over the early space program. I resolved to be respectful.

Bill was first to greet the governor, who was by then in a wheelchair as a result of an assassination attempt in 1972 during his failed presidential campaign. Bill addressed him as "Judge," and I recalled he had been a circuit court judge early in his career. When it was my turn to be introduced, I bent over to see him eye-to-eye. He had large lips and terrible dandruff, plus he smelled of cigar smoke and alcohol. I thought, *My god! He looks like a corpse.* As he reached over and shook my hand, his handler repositioned his wheelchair and rolled directly over my toes. I couldn't hold back a yelp, which created an awkward moment. The handler briskly moved Governor Wallace on.

I attended the rally as an observer of history, and even though it was a disappointment, I ended up meeting a person of historical status. Wallace went on to win his historical fourth and final term. By the time of the rally in 1982, he had come to terms with the fact that he had been on the wrong side of history with his divisive civil rights stance; however, he lived a tormented retirement, arguing that he was not a racist in his heart. He died in 1998 at the age of seventy-nine. Years later when I saw the movie, *Forrest Gump* and the "stand in the schoolhouse door" scene, I was reminded of my serendipitous encounter with George Wallace.

Alabama Governor George Wallace

I developed a close relationship with my parents during those years. We ate dinner together every evening, and they stayed and helped until the job was complete. Steve helped out for a while, but after he met Gaby, an attractive college student and the daughter of our parents' friends, there was little time for the family business. She grew up a "military brat" in Germany, and because Steve had been stationed there for three years with the Army, they had a lot in common. Following a short courtship our family reunited to attend their small intimate wedding in Huntsville in August 1982. I was Steve's best man, and during the lighting of the unity candle, I performed on the guitar and sang "If," a love song popularized by the group, Bread. Susan and her husband, Morris, who was a police officer in the Muscle Shoals area, attended with their two-year-old daughter, Jennifer and two-month-old son, Ryan. At the time, Lori was working for a telecommunications company in Indianapolis and Debbie was leaving her job as a reporter for the Columbus (Ohio) Citizen-Journal newspaper for a new position as press secretary to the former astronaut John Glenn in his campaign for president of the United States. Glenn began his career as a decorated Marine pilot and then was a top Navy test pilot before volunteering for the NASA orbital program. On February 20, 1962, Glenn stepped into the role of American hero when he piloted the first manned space mission aboard the Mercury-Atlas 6 Friendship 7, becoming the first American to orbit the earth. By the 1970s, he had turned his attention to politics, and in 1974, Ohio elected him senator. Debbie's introduction to politics would lead her in 1984 to the job of press secretary for Ohio Governor Richard Celeste.

Family reunited at Steve's wedding
(front row l to r: Gaby, Jennifer, Morris, Susan holding Ryan, Lori)
(back row l to r: Steve, Scott, Mom, Dad, Brad, Debbie, Tom)

I remember how proud and excited I was for Debbie. I clearly saw our shared passion. We had a desire to attach ourselves to something larger than ourselves. I was happy that she would have a connection with the space program and I secretly hoped that I would have an opportunity to meet Senator Glenn someday.

Steve was also working on the lightweight tank at MSFC. When the External Tank production at Michoud began staffing up, Steve deemed it a more lucrative opportunity and applied for a job transfer. We shared an apartment, and because of the anticipated relocation, we continued the current living arrangement after he and Gaby were married. Three of us living together in tight quarters quickly became awkward and contentious. We were all relieved when the transfer was approved and they moved to New Orleans a few months later.

I continued to be motivated and willing to work hard to see my parent's business become a success. It was all worth it when my dad finally bought his first new car—a red Cadillac—five years later.

United Mailing

Comprehensive mailing services for local, regional and national mailers of any size

U nited Mailing is a family owned business that considers complete customer satisfaction their most important objective. "No matter what it takes, our main objective is to provide service to our clients to the very best of our ability," says owner Dick Phillips. "Our customers trust us with their mailing needs."

United Mailing is the largest, most technologically advanced mailing company in North Alabama. Also known as a letter shop and bulk mailing company, their mailing services include the capability to mail first class pre-sort, second class or third class bulk mail. Plus, they now specialize in international mailings.

The staff and equipment at United Mailing can accomodate almost any type or size mailer, from local or regional, to national or international in scope.

Dick Phillips will encourage anyone to call one of United Mailing's many satisfied customers for a testimonial of how pleased they are with the full range of services.

United Mailing is a strong believer in building and maintaining trust with their clients; a quality they have clearly proven. You can trust United Mailing to cost-effectively handle all your mailing needs and you can be sure it will be done according to your time schedule, specifications and budget.

4411-C Evangel Circle
Huntsville, AL 35816

Mon. - Fri.   7:00 am - 4:30 pm

837 - 2100

The staff at United Mailing

Dad's first new car

Woodism

*Action with a vision turned out to be
a good decision.*

Challenger and Beyond

In 1982, after the testing phase, Scooter, Bob Stowell, and Steve took positions in New Orleans on the production phase of the program. The Shuttle Program was a ground floor opportunity with the anticipation that as tank production increased, promotions would follow. Initially, six heavyweight tanks were produced and used. As a way to cut costs and increase payloads, NASA tasked us with reducing the external tank by 6,000 pounds, down from 76,000 pounds dry weight. For each pound of weight reduced off the tank, a pound of payload could be increased—including crew, supplies, oxygen, and satellites.

Even as Steve and Gaby were starting their life together in New Orleans, Steve was also adjusting to a work situation with a new twist: It was in a union environment. He hadn't anticipated the challenges that would cause. Steve was always a get-it-done sort of guy, and his temperament was not compatible with being told, "Oh no, you can't do it that way." As soon as he fulfilled his one-year obligation in New Orleans, he and Gaby jumped at the chance to return to Huntsville with the Shuttle Program. Even though the position was a step backward, it was worth being back in his familiar work environment and closer to family.

During this time, Martin Marietta and Boeing were developing mock-ups at MSFC and bidding on the new Space Station Program. Boeing proposed that all production work would take place in Huntsville, while Martin Marietta chose Denver, Colorado, as their production site. The principle decision-makers were located in Huntsville, and Steve felt sure that Boeing would be awarded the contract. He saw this as a greater opportunity and decided to jump to the competitor. Boeing subsequently did win the Space Station contract. It was a colossal mistake, I believe, by Martin Marietta to not bid production in Huntsville.

Martin Marietta's full-scale functional model of a Space Station module

Due to my family obligations, I chose not to move to New Orleans after the testing phase. It was a difficult period for me. The new lightweight tank program presented an environment that was extremely dirty, noisy, and physically confining. It involved cutting metal, testing, cutting metal, testing—over and over. I missed my old team. I missed the camaraderie and friendships that had been forged over twelve-hour days, seven days a week—and the endless nightshift shenanigans. I wanted to stay with the program, but I needed more challenge and autonomy. I decided it was time to do something different. I looked toward a career move.

An opportunity soon presented itself when Henry Hankal came into my life. Henry was a grizzled former army master sergeant who had specialized in logistics in North Africa during World War II. He was a heavy drinker, smoked like a chimney, and had a strong resemblance to the 1930s actor Tyrone Power. He retired in 1965 after twenty-five years of military service and went on to private industry with Martin Marietta in 1977. Henry managed the Logistics department for Martin Marietta at MSFC.

Our relationship began in 1983 when I volunteered to sit in for Henry while he was out of the office for a couple weeks following surgery. When he returned, his health issues made the physical responsibilities of the job a struggle. He needed a part-time employee with a strong back to help him out. I volunteered and began to split my time between logistics and working technical issues on the lightweight tank. I found that I enjoyed working logistics—particularly having autonomy and the ability to interface with employees at all levels of NASA.

I could tell Henry liked me. We would have hearty conversations over lunch, and it just sort of clicked for us. He enjoyed talking about World War II—stories of atrocities and mistreatment that I didn't really want to hear, but he had a way of imparting lessons along the way. He would ask, "What would you do in this situation?" I usually flunked the test, but he continued to guide my thinking. He often said, "You're not really living in the real world, Scott." When he was my age, he had seen and experienced things—things I hoped I would never have to experience. Over time, he began to trust me as a confidant. His life lessons invariably caused me to pause and think about the intricate aspects of life and human nature.

We occasionally talked about what-ifs and what my future would look like in Logistics. It would involve procurement and managing the transportation and property management of flight hardware and test equipment. What I mostly heard was promotional opportunities, autonomy, flexibility, a company vehicle, job security, a clean environment, and an opportunity to meet people—lots of people. I sensed that he was looking for the right person to mentor, someone he could pass his legacy on to. I suspected he had his eye out for a Vietnam veteran, but at the time, those guys were few and far between.

By 1984, the production phase of the External Tank Program was in full swing, growing from 45 to 150 employees; my part-time position in Logistics turned into a full-time opening. I decided to transfer. You could say that the role of logistics engineer found me. This was the road I was destined to take, and Henry Hankal became my mentor.

Our relationship also grew outside of work. He would occasionally invite me to his home on the weekends for a home-cooked meal; in turn, I gladly helped him with odd jobs around his house. We continued our lively conversations off the clock. We discussed—and debated—human nature long into the evenings over a couple straight-up glasses of scotch or a bottle of wine. That's where I first heard the term *in vino veritas*, which means, "In wine, there is truth." Henry had an inviting bar setup in his home, and he enjoyed the friendship—and being the bartender.

Scott and Henry

Henry challenged me at every turn. He was well read and especially enjoyed reading historical literature. He was articulate and loved to use analogies. To this day, I find myself using them to explain a point. I also learned the art of philosophical conversation from Henry. He once told me, "Everything in life is connected in some way. What separates humankind is our memories and our experiences. No two memories or experiences are alike."

At times, it appeared he took pleasure in exposing my weaknesses. We had a love/hate relationship. In a sense, he sort of became my "at-work father." He offered me constructive criticism, and I accepted his help. He would mark in his calendar everything that he asked me to do and then throw it up in my face if it wasn't completed on time. He often baited me, and he liked to quiz me on tasks. He knew I was very intuitive and would challenge me to locate a file folder by instinct.

Logistics requires a high level of discipline. You are measured by results. There was no guesswork allowed; everything had to be precisely accurate. I always described it as: You may not know what I do, but when I don't do it, you'll know! Henry taught me the correct lingo and the importance of speaking precisely. It was important that the people I interacted with trusted what I said. I had to learn the art of gaining others' confidence. He would say, "Don't ever say, 'I think,' and don't commit to things you're not 100 percent sure about." I was grateful to Henry for his mentoring and for the skills I learned.

These lessons were the best education I could have gotten— things they can't, or at least don't, teach you in college. I built a career on them. I learned the importance of not overreacting and how to put myself in other people's shoes. I learned to be diplomatic in dealing with situations and to think on my feet, to be solution-oriented. Ultimately, I learned how to make things happen. I found my own unique brand and treated everyone as part of the team, from the janitors to the truck drivers to my coworkers to NASA administration. I strived to be genuine.

Early 1986 was a turning point for Henry. We were beginning to automate the logistics function through a mainframe computer located at the Huntsville Operations Support Center (HOSC). We'd enter our data on a keyboard at our desks and then drive a half-mile to the HOSC to pick up the printout. Henry wanted no part in the transition. He was perfectly happy with his pencil-and-paper system.

On the cold Tuesday morning of January 28, 1986, I was driving to work, excited that Steve was bringing his newborn daughter, Ashley, home from the hospital. I was also eager to check the status of the Space Shuttle Challenger. This was an historic flight for a couple of reasons. From the point of view of the program, it was the first launching of a Shuttle from Pad 39B; the last time that pad had been used was for the Apollo Soyuz in 1975. With the anticipated increase in flights and the need for an additional launch pad, major upgrades had been made to prepare it for the Shuttle, including a white room with an arm to allow satellites to be loaded in the orbiter payload and a "beanie cap" to vent the external forward oxygen tank prior to lift off.

To the average American, the flight was of greater significance due to the NASA Teacher in Space Project, a program announced by President Ronald Reagan in 1984 to inspire student interest in mathematics, science, and space exploration. Christa McAuliffe, a 38-year-old high-school social studies teacher and mother of two from New Hampshire, was selected from more than 11,000 project applicants to be the first school teacher in space. The announcement was made with great fanfare during a ceremony at the White House.

As a member of the mission, McAuliffe trained at the Johnson Space Center and planned to conduct experiments and teach two lessons from space. Excitement for the space program was at an all-time high, and the American public, including millions of school-aged children, were watching on that historic morning. McAuliffe's parents, husband, children, and friends were among the audience at Kennedy Space Center to witness the Challenger lift-off.

As with every other launch, I looked forward to viewing it on the monitor near my office. It was due to lift off around lunchtime, and I had planned my morning around it. My first stop was at NASA Contracts Office, where I learned that they were preparing to sign a new contract with Martin Marietta for the External Tank. It would be the largest single contract issued to date, requiring us to build twenty-four tanks per year and employ nearly 5,000 people at our Michoud facility in New Orleans. These were truly exciting times.

Then our office received an urgent request for parts needed for a critical test that morning. I had to pick them up and was disappointed that this would be the first launch I would miss watching in real time. My new responsibilities in Logistics left me with no other choice. Besides, the flight had already scrubbed several times, and I was fairly certain it would be scrubbed once again due to the cold weather.

I had my van radio tuned in to a local station as I drove the ten miles to our vendor, Machine Craft, to pick up the parts. Halfway there, an announcer broke into the programming to report, "The Shuttle launched moments ago, and NASA has lost its downlink to the Shuttle." I felt a wave of nausea as I thought about what this might mean. Without a phone or way to communicate, I sped to Machine Craft, desperate to call the office.

I entered their facility and saw a TV tuned to CNN's coverage of the event. Phones were ringing, and there was urgent activity, including locking the doors. I knew that all parts, records, and test data from first- and second-tier vendors would be immediately impounded pending an investigation. I called Henry, who told me, "The Shuttle exploded. You better get back here." I don't remember driving the ten miles back to MSFC. I had the radio on, but I was numb, completely devastated.

Challenger Mission 51-L Disaster. Courtesy NASA

There was no way to know yet if the explosion was due to equipment failure or terrorism, so security was unusually tight getting back on to MSFC. They checked badges and license plates.

In the office, as we watched CNN replay the same moments over and over, we were in anguish, our hearts aching for the families of the seven lost crew members: Commander Dick Scobee; Pilot Michael Smith; Mission Specialists Ellison Onizuka (the first Asian-American in space), Judith Resnik (the second female astronaut) and Ronald McNair (the second African-American in space); and Payload Specialists Gregory Jarvis and McAuliffe.

Our phones rang incessantly. Rumors were already flying about what had caused the accident. The External Tank? The three main engines? The Solid Rocket Boosters? I wasn't surprised when I received calls with such questions as, "Do you think the External Tank was responsible for the accident?" and "Do you think the tank lost integrity after 10,000 pounds were shaved from the ring frame?" Tony Andreoni, our Huntsville operations director, quickly gathered us together. "Do not talk to the press," he told us. "Refer all calls to the public affairs office." We began to consider what this incident could mean to the entire program—and to us.

One week later, on February 6, President Reagan appointed the Rogers Commission to investigate and determine the cause of the accident. Ad hoc committees representing all Shuttle elements were formed at MSFC to establish a path forward. I was Logistics point of contact, coordinating critical test data for the External Tank with our Michoud facility. I also provided engineering and materials support to the NASA team. A month later, when films from the accident were released, it was obvious that the O-ring surrounding the solid rocket booster was the cause of the explosion. But we would still have to wait for release of the final report from the Rogers Commission.

Rogers Commission principals. Courtesy Rogers Commission Report

It was an awkward time for Henry and me. We shared an office and our desks faced each other. We were in high gear following the Challenger accident. Henry and I would arrive at work, and my phone would immediately start ringing with requests. Henry's remained quiet. I would hear, "Scott, I need your help. We need it today—not tomorrow." Henry was experiencing poor health, and it seemed that the fire in the belly was flickering out. I was diplomatic and made sure not to undermine him, but the physical work had to be done. We were moving at such a fast pace and I became the go-to guy to make sure things happened—and quickly. It was a necessary part of the transition process, but tensions increased between us.

Henry held back as long as he could. One day, after a conversation about the tasks facing us for the day, he let loose. The look on his face was one of a broken man. He lashed out at me with every cuss word he knew. I came close to walking out at that moment, but I loved my job and I realized there was still much more Henry had to teach me. I knew my future was on this path. I took a deep breath and let him vent. We never spoke of that morning again.

The Challenger accident proved to be too much for Henry, both emotionally and physically. He decided it was time to retire. We had worked together for a couple of years, and I felt very confident in the position because of his mentoring. I hoped that I would be selected to replace him. I guess Henry was confident as well. He said, "Tony is interviewing several candidates for the position, but I want you to know that I have recommended you for the job." And fortunately, I was selected. Tony Andreoni took a chance with me, and I am forever grateful.

Henry retired from Martin Marietta in May 1986. As he walked out the door, with a cigarette dangling from his mouth, he said to me, "You have what I've given you. Keep your nose clean and don't screw it up!" For two years, coworkers called me Hankal Junior. As the saying goes, "Build off the shoulders of giants."

Scott and Tony Andreoni

For the first six months after the Challenger accident, I was on call 24/7. Martin Marietta ran endless tank tests at the Michoud Facility and I would occasionally find myself on the Huntsville Airport tarmac in the middle of the night, receiving reams of data from Michoud to deliver to the ad hoc committee so they could report test results to the Rogers Commission. It was a difficult time, but during the investigation, I had the honor and privilege of meeting many of the Rogers Commission principals including Neil Armstrong, Sally Ride, and William Rogers, who had been the secretary of state under Richard Nixon.

The long hours, on top of Henry transitioning into retirement, made it a trial-by-fire experience. Logistics responsibilities began to transfer to me. I became the point of contact for all logistics supporting the External Tank element. But the new contract was put on hold indefinitely, never to be signed. Through it all, my duties with my parents' business continued. At least, I had youth on my side. It was a very demanding time in my life, both physically and emotionally, and even Henry couldn't prepare me for what was coming down the road. There was no roadmap for a full-blown disaster such as the Challenger accident. It stretched me beyond what I could have imagined.

The Rogers Commission completed their investigation on June 6, 1986. It reported that the ground temperature at launch was 36 degrees, which was 15 degrees colder than that of any previous launch. Just after liftoff, photographic data showed a strong puff of gray smoke spurting from the vicinity of the aft field joint on the right Solid Rocket Booster. The vaporized material streaming from the joint indicated there was not complete sealing action within the joint. That area of the Solid Rocket Booster faced the External Tank.

Photos depicting ice on Pad 39B morning of launch. Courtesy NASA

Arrow points to puff of gray smoke escaping from failed
O-ring joint during launch. Courtesy NASA

The Space Shuttle Challenger on Mission 51-L began at
11:38 a.m. EST on January 28, 1986, and ended 73 seconds later
in an explosive burn of hydrogen and oxygen propellants that
destroyed the External Tank and exposed the Orbiter to severe
aerodynamic loads, causing complete structural breakup. The two
Solid Rocket Boosters flew out of the fireball and were destroyed
by the Air Force range safety officer 110 seconds after launch.

Solid Rocket Booster flying out of the fireball. Courtesy NASA

Burnthrough of the right Solid Rocket Booster
aft field joint. Courtesy NASA

The pressurized or non-pressurized External Tank structural elements that could cause structural failure were examined in detail. All construction, structural test data, test inspection records, and x-rays were reviewed. The commission concluded that no structural imperfections existed that could have created a leak or caused catastrophic failure of the External Tank (ET-26).

All propulsion elements, including the three main engines and Solid Rocket Boosters, were managed at MSFC. Prior to Challenger, an autocratic management style existed within NASA that did not want to hear bad news. There was a lot of pressure on the contractors to maintain schedules and not hold up launches. I was reminded that a program is as strong as its weakest link and how one wrong decision can bring down an entire program.

Although it stretched me to my limit, the experience seasoned me in Logistics. I was no longer called Hankal Jr. I guess you could say the "green" had finally ripened. Henry had taught me the unique art form of logistics, and I developed my unique style, which included perseverance, patience, a positive attitude, diplomacy, enthusiasm, and a hands-on approach. I never asked anything of anyone that I would not do myself. I had the privilege of working with many key players in the Shuttle Program. The position was high profile and afforded me high exposure—which could be good and bad! I was successful in turning a somewhat routine job into something special.

Hankal, Jr. post-Challenger

Two years post-Challenger

I had the NASA photo lab enlarge a photograph of the Challenger crew to 16- by 20-inches. It hung on my office wall for the rest of my career, serving as a constant reminder of how unforgiving human space flight can be.

Challenger crew of Mission 51-L. Courtesy NASA

Following the Rogers Commission recommendations, NASA felt it had a clear mandate going forward. Our team supported MSFC facility modifications, a redesign of the Solid Rocket Boosters and enhancements to the External Tank that provided redundancy systems in case of failure. After thirty-three months, our efforts were successful. We returned to flight with STS-26 on the Orbiter, Discovery, in the fall of 1988, and the crew later visited MSFC for a Return to Flight Celebration.

We were excited to be rebuilding back to the future; however, after Challenger, the Michoud tank production decreased dramatically. We ended up losing more than 1,000 of our Michoud employees during those thirty-three months, and tank production was cut to a snail's pace, averaging four tanks per year. We were hopeful that the program would build back to its original flight rate after President Reagan authorized a replacement Orbiter.

Return to Flight on STS-26. Courtesy NASA

The Rogers Commission recommended that the Shuttle no longer fly commercial payloads due to the reliance on the Shuttle as the main space launch capability. This had created a relentless pressure on NASA to increase the flight rate and pressure on the contractors to maintain the launch schedules. In light of that recommendation, President Reagan signed an executive order ensuring that no commercial payloads would be flown going forward.

President Reagan got it right when he said, "The future is not free: the story of all human progress is one of a struggle against all odds. We learned again that this America, which Abraham Lincoln called the last, best hope of man on Earth, was built on heroism and noble sacrifice. It was built by men and women like our seven star voyagers, who answered a call beyond duty, who gave more than was expected or required and who gave it little thought of worldly reward."

After Henry retired, I visited him in Tennessee. He predicted that if I remained in Logistics, I would be one of the last people out the door when and if the Shuttle Program ended. He also predicted that I would enjoy my independence and autonomy, but he also foresaw my pain. He said, "You will not be appreciated and, at times, you will be abused in your position."

The greatest gift Henry gave me was the lessons from the poem "Desiderata," written in 1927 by Max Ehrmann. Henry carried it with him in World War II, and when he retired, he gave me his original copy. I kept it posted on my office wall and found solace in its sage advice during stressful times at work and passed it along whenever appropriate.

DESIDERATA:

GO PLACIDLY AMID THE NOISE & HASTE, & REMEMBER WHAT PEACE THERE MAY BE IN SILENCE. AS FAR AS POSSIBLE WHITHOUT SURRENDER, BE ON GOOD TERMS WITH ALL PERSONS. SPEAK YOUR TRUTH QUIETLY & CLEARLY; AND LISTEN TO OTHERS, EVEN THE DULL & IGNORANT; THEY TOO HAVE THEIR STORY. AVOID LOUD & AGRESSIVE PERSONS, THEY ARE VEXATIONS TO THE SPIRIT. IF YOU COMPARE YOURSELF TO OTHERS, YOU MAY BECOME VAIN & BITTER; FOR ALWAYS THERE WILL BE GREATER & LESSER PERSONS THAN YOURSELF. ENJOY YOUR ACHIEVEMENTS AS WELL AS YOUR PLANS. KEEP INTERESTED IN YOUR OWN CAREER, HOWEVER HUMBLE; IT IS A REAL POSSESSION IN THE CHANGING FORTUNES OF TIME. EXCERCISE CAUTION IN YOUR BUSINESS AFFAIRS; FOR THE WORLD IS FULL OF TRICKERY. BUT LET THIS NOT BLIND YOU TO WHAT VIRTUE THERE IS; MANY PERSONS STRIVE FOR HIGH IDEALS; AND EVERYWHERE LIFE IS FULL OF HEROISM. BE YOURSELF. ESPECIALLY, DO NOT FEIGN AFFECTION. NEITHER BE CYNICAL ABOUT LOVE; FOR IN THE FACE OF ALL ARIDITY & DISENCHANTMENT IT IS PERENNIAL AS THE GRASS. TAKE KINDLY THE COUNSEL OF THE YEARS, GRACEFULLY SURRENDERING THE THINGS OF YOUTH. NURTURE STRENGTH OF SPIRIT TO SHIELD YOU IN SUDDEN MISFORTUNE. BUT DO NOT DISTRESS YOURSELF WITH IMAGININGS. MANY FEARS ARE BORN OF FATIGUE & LONELINESS. BEYOND A WHOLESOME DISCIPLINE, BE GENTLY WITH YOURSELF. YOU ARE A CHILD OF THE UNIVERSE, NO LESS THAN THE TREES & THE STARS; YOU HAVE A RIGHT TO BE HERE. AND WHETHER OR NOT IS IS CLEAR TO YOU, NO DOUBT THE UNIVERSE IS UNFOLDING AS IT SHOULD. THEREFORE, BE AT PEACE WITH GOD, WHATEVER YOU CONCEIVE HIM TO BE, AND WHATEVER YOUR LABORS & ASPIRATIONS, IN THE NOISY CONFUSION OF LIFE KEEP PEACE WITH YOUR SOUL. WITH ALL ITS SHAM, DRUDGERY & BROKEN DREAMS, IT IS STILL A BEAUTIFUL WORLD. BE CAREFUL. STRIVE TO BE HAPPY......

FOUND IN OLD SAINT PAUL'S CHURCH,BALTIMORE, DATED 1692.....

The Desiderata poem that hung on my office wall

Henry's health continued to fail and by 1997, he required continuous oxygen due to his years of heavy smoking. Later that year, his wife, Mary, telephoned to let me know that Henry had passed away.

My last visit to Henry's home in Tennessee

Woodism

I believe it is our nature as human beings to listen to those who don't actually want to help us and ignore the ones who do...I'm glad I listened.

Successes, Failures, and Near Misses

Every city has important, unique landmarks that help to define it. A major historical attraction in Huntsville, Alabama, is the Space and Rocket Center, a museum of hundreds of space-related artifacts and memorabilia. In 1988, the city skyline and the museum itself got a stunning addition when the first External Tank—the Main Propulsion Test Article (MPTA)—became part of a full-scale Space Shuttle stack on permanent loan from NASA.

After ten and a half years at the Stennis Space Center in Bay St. Louis, Mississippi, supporting the Shuttle main engine testing, the tank was prepared for its final journey to the Center. While people were celebrating Mardi Gras in the streets of New Orleans on February 16, a team of Martin Marietta employees removed the tank from the test stand and transported it by open barge to Michoud, where it was transferred to a covered barge called Orion before heading up the Mississippi River to Huntsville. The 1,250-mile journey along the Mississippi, Ohio, and Tennessee rivers took twelve days.

MPTA tank on covered Orion barge. Courtesy NASA

MPTA tank on its transporter at MSFC preparing
to offload from Orion. Courtesy NASA

I was the logistics point of contact responsible for transporting
the tank from the Orion to MSFC and then on to its current
home at the Space and Rocket Center. Planning was enormous
and far-reaching. The other principals in this effort were Tony

Andreoni, my director, and Homer Gray, our planner. As we prepared to move the tank to Building 4705 at MSFC, where it would undergo modifications, we realized that the tank was 39.5 feet high and the bay opening was 40 feet. We released air from the tires of the transporter to ensure a smooth entry. Our next priority was to install I-beam spokes inside the tank to support the 89-ton test Orbiter Pathfinder, which would be mounted on top.

MPTA tank entering Building 4705 at MSFC

Installation of I-beam spokes in the tank

The logistical details of the move to the Center's outdoor display were monumental and had to be exact. By moving day, our team had calculated every inch of the route from Building 4705 at MSFC to the Space and Rocket Center—a six-mile journey the MPTA tank would travel on a specially built transporter. We arranged for military police escorts and shut down major thoroughfares. It was a very big deal.

MPTA tank with military escort

Everything went according to plan—well almost. We arrived at the Space and Rocket Center and had the display area in sight. But to get to it, we had to make a sweeping 90-degree turn. To our surprise, we realized that, because of the length of the tank and the degree of the turn, the tank would run right into a tree, which had, obviously, been on that spot for many years.

MPTA tank meets tree

Prior to our arrival, a path of heavy gravel and stone had been laid, so we were unable to deviate from the route. After some calculations and a team huddle, we decided we had two plausible options: One was to lift the tank with a crane, which would mean a major financial and time setback; the other was to request permission to cut down the tree. Of course, we chose the second option. Ed Buckbee, the director of the Space and Rocket Center, granted us permission, and we took a chainsaw to the tree. Those who knew me understood my personal pain from cutting it down.

Completion of the display was then slightly delayed when it was discovered that sixty-five of the eighty-nine tons of the Orbiter Pathfinder were concentrated in the tail. We had to add more support inside the External Tank so it would hold the added weight.

MPTA mounted with added support

Orbiter Pathfinder being mounted on MPTA tank. Courtesy NASA

The MPTA is currently mated to the Pathfinder and two pre-Challenger excessed filament-wound solid rocket booster casings as a complete Shuttle stack at the Space and Rocket Center. It is the only display of its kind and has become an iconic landmark in the Huntsville skyline. Without exception, whenever I pass it, I'm reminded of the day we installed the MPTA with some real-time adjustments. This display is important not only to our community, but it also is the inspiration for the Shuttle model configurations that I am known for today.

Iconic full Shuttle stack configuration located at the Space and Rocket Center in Huntsville, AL. Courtesy NASA

After the Challenger disaster, we were at a snail's pace, assembling only three or four tanks a year. NASA and Martin Marietta were looking at ways to maintain skilled workers for future production increases. With the expectation of success and NASA funding, we experimented with a number of forward-thinking plans that would use the External Tank for multipurpose functions and complement the Space Transportation System.

External Tanks had been used only on Shuttle flights and were discarded just before reaching orbit. The first major experiment I managed for Martin Marietta Logistics was the Gamma Ray Imaging Telescope (GRIT). This was exciting work, as we believed gamma rays would provide information about some of the most energetic phenomena in the universe. The possibilities for this project were enormous and, if successful, would lay the groundwork for gamma ray detectors to screen merchant ship containers as they entered our country, and gamma radiation to sterilize medical equipment, remove decay-causing bacteria from foods, and the potential to treat certain types of cancer.

Gamma Ray Imaging Telescope mock up in Building 4705 at MSFC

NASA awarded a contract to study the feasibility of outfitting an External Tank on orbit as a GRIT. Components of the GRIT were to be carried in the Shuttle's cargo bay. Instead of dropping the tank eight minutes after launch, it would remain attached to the Orbiter and the leftover fuels would carry it into orbit. Once in space, astronauts would assemble telescope components within the tank section. It would then be pressurized to provide the needed environment for the gamma ray detection technique.

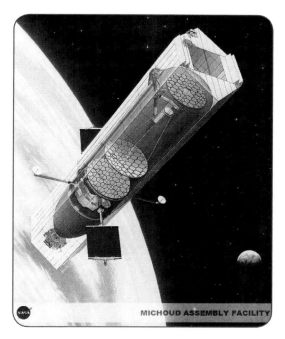

Proposed Gamma Ray Imaging Telescope

We built a mock-up to evaluate a reconfiguration of the tank for the GRIT system and placed it in the MSFC Neutral Buoyancy Simulator, which was in the building next to my office. The simulator was a pool of water 40 feet deep and 75 feet wide, holding 1,300,000 gallons of water. It offered an environment similar to the zero-gravity of space by floating people and test hardware. This was the first time that astronauts would have access entry to the External Tank. They suited up, collected their tools and equipment, and entered the tank through the 36-inch manhole cover. The entire concept of the GRIT depended on the capabilities of astronauts to perform required tasks within the External Tank in a safe and timely manner.

Astronaut training in the Neutral Bouyancy Simulator. Courtesy NASA

One of the astronauts who came to train at the Neutral Buoyancy Simulator was Bruce McCandless, a former Navy pilot who had flown on the tenth Shuttle mission, during which he performed the first ever untethered walk in space using a manned maneuvering unit (MMU). Because everyone knew of my propensity for collecting memorabilia and autographs, word got out that I wanted to meet him. One day, as I was sitting at my desk, I heard a knock on my door and saw Bruce standing there with a big grin on his face. I was disappointed at first that I didn't have anything for him to autograph, but then I remembered a calendar with his famous spacewalk photo. He gladly signed it, and we talked shop for almost an hour. I couldn't help asking, "What was the MMU solo experience like?" His eyes lit up. "It was so fantastic. I felt like a human satellite with the world at me feet," he said. "That experience topped my career!" We talked about the future of the GRIT, and he was excited about the project. "I see that as my next challenge, and the MMU is a perfect application," he said. "We could fly over from the Shuttle and harness the External Tank like a horse."

Astronaut Bruce McCandless performing untethered extra-vehicular activity (EVA) with the MMU on STS-41B. Courtesy NASA

The Gamma Ray Imaging Telescope was proven to be a doable project and offered incredible possibilities in medicine and national security, but unfortunately, due to budget constraints, it never came to fruition. We felt it was a missed opportunity for our country considering the innovations that could have been achieved. And I believe no one was more disappointed than Bruce McCandless.

Another exciting project under development was designed to reduce the costs and risks associated with the Orbiter and crew. NASA awarded a contract to develop a heavy-lift vehicle called Shuttle-C (for cargo), using existing Shuttle hardware—engines, boosters, external tank—and launch facilities. The Orbiter would be replaced by an unmanned cargo element with increased payload capacity and eliminate the risk to human flight crews.

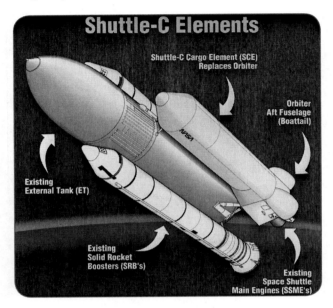

Graphic of Shuttle-C elements

The principle purpose was to see if the Shuttle-C would be cost-effective for carrying large elements of the future Space Station. If it proved to be viable, it would be able to lift 100,000 to 150,000 pounds into orbit and would free the Space Shuttle for increased work in all sciences, including solar-system exploration, astronomy, life sciences, and materials-processing experimentation. Progress in all of these areas had been severely constrained by the Challenger accident.

It was fascinating to watch the Shuttle-C being constructed right outside my office door. I spent a lot of time climbing around the model and took pictures at each stage of development. I watched it grow from a concept to a high-fidelity model. Over time, I came to know every square inch of the Shuttle-C mock-up. Unfortunately, once again, due to NASA's budget constraints— and to everyone's shock—the entire program was cancelled.

Shuttle-C mock-up under construction

Completed Shuttle-C mock-up

The Shuttle-C mock-up remained in place as a Space and Rocket Center exhibit and part of the NASA bus tour. I was flabbergasted that the project didn't fly, but because of my enthusiasm for everything related to the Space Shuttle, I was called upon numerous times to provide tours of the Shuttle-C. Later, the mock-up, too, was disassembled and eventually scrapped.

Another project set in motion with the goal of reducing weight and increasing safety was the redesign of the External Tank nose cone. To the casual observer, the nose cone was the pointed arch shape at the top of the external tank. With its pencil-shaped point, it helped to reduce aerodynamic drag during the Shuttle's ascent and carried a lightning rod to ground a potential strike. The only time the world noticed the nose cone was when the "beanie cap" was retracted from the top of the tank two minutes before launch. In reality, the 56.5-inch diameter nose cone, used as a cover for the very sophisticated liquid oxygen venting system, was the only flight-certified hardware component for the External Tank manufactured in Huntsville. It was classified "Critical 1," meaning that failure to perform could cause loss of vehicle and crew. It was always very special to us because it was at the apex of the Shuttle stack and the first element to leave the launch pad, proving itself time and again.

Nose cone with "beanie cap." Courtesy NASA

When the first 89 shuttles launched, the External Tanks flew with metallic nose cones covered with thermal insulation.

In 1985, for the purpose of increasing safety and trimming weight from the External Tank, and through a collaboration with NASA, our team investigated reducing and eliminating some components of the thermal insulation. As with all weight reductions of the External Tank, the result would be an increase in Shuttle payload capacity.

However, after a near miss with major tile damage to Space Shuttle Atlantis, which occurred during the STS-27 mission in December 1988, an initiative to redesign the nose cone to help reduce foam loss from the External Tank was accelerated. STS-27 was the second post-Challenger mission carrying a top-secret military spy satellite. The flight became a frightening close call that had the potential to bring the Shuttle Program to an early end. Commander Robert "Hoot" Gibson and crewmates Mike Mullane, Guy Gardner, Jerry Ross, and William Shepherd saw images of tile damage on TV monitors in the cockpit, but had no idea that Atlantis had been hit during ascent.

Upon reviewing launch film, the ground team determined there had been a strike from the right-hand Solid Rocket Booster insulation. The following day, mission control called up with a request to use Atlantis' robot arm to inspect the Shuttle's heat shield on the Orbiter's right side. The arm was maneuvered into position so a black-and-white television camera could see the tiles in question. It appeared that hundreds of tiles had been damaged. If even one of those tiles had been penetrated, reentry would have been a catastrophic breakup of the Orbiter.

Because it was a classified Department of Defense mission, military restrictions prevented the crew from downlinking pictures or television images showing the chipped and broken tiles. They had to send encrypted TV that produced frames about every three seconds. The astronauts anxiously waited for mission control's assessment. When they heard, "We've looked at the images, and mechanical says it's not a problem. The damage isn't that severe," they were stunned. The analysis on the ground determined that the astronauts had been misled by poor lighting conditions and grainy TV images.

The crew knew better. The images were crystal clear on the Shuttle and definitely alarming. "Houston, we're seeing a lot of damage," confirmed Gibson. But mission control repeated the engineering assessment that the damage was not that severe. The astronauts reluctantly accepted the judgment of mission control and acquiesced. It wasn't clear what, if anything, could have been done if engineers had realized the severity of the problem. There were no tile repair tools on board the Shuttle and no techniques for even getting an astronaut to the damage site. Changes to the Shuttle's reentry orientation and trajectory could have been attempted, but even that was an unknown.

As it turned out, Atlantis did not suffer a burn-through, and Gibson guided the Shuttle to a smooth landing. After touchdown, the crew, engineers, and NASA management gathered on the runway and were astonished at what they saw. The damage was much worse than even the crew expected. A thorough examination revealed 700 damaged tiles extending along half of Atlantis' length. Post investigation determined that they were within millimeters of a burn-through. They were very lucky. It was further determined that the encrypted video resolution was poor and an incorrect conclusion was reached. It was the most extensive Shuttle heat shield damage recorded to date.

Subsequent studies were conducted, and it was predicted that the External Tank metallic nose cone thermal insulation posed a hazard to the Orbiter heat shield tiles and to the windshield, which could crack or shatter, exposing the crew to aerodynamic forces beyond their control.

NASA ET Projects Office at MSFC decided that the elimination of the potential debris, increasing reliability, and reducing weight and the number of manufacturing parts required to build the nose cone was a high priority. The metallic nose cone was replaced with a graphite composite shell that could withstand the heat during launch, which reached 1,100 degree F. Without the need for insulation, it was much safer and 10 pounds lighter.

Metallic nose cone used on the first 89 External Tanks

Composite nose cone on External Tank

Over time, our facility was transformed from research and development (R&D) to one that produced flight hardware. With the one-piece "monocoque" composite shell, we eliminated the need for some 50 parts and more than 1,000 fasteners, thus increasing reliability.

In the early '90s, several technical issues had developed during R&D and the composite nose cone project was in serious jeopardy. We were tasked with resolving materials and curing issues while continuing to fly the metallic nose cones. I was the designated Logistics point of contact, representing Huntsville at the Michoud facility, and was responsible for presenting the tracking system information for manufacturing parts and elements, storage, composite temperature-control issues, and materials management. I had a comprehensive plan for everything, except one major issue. During the planning meeting, I raised my hand and asked, "How will we handle damaged or non-accepted nose cones due to manufacturing defects?" The room fell unnervingly silent. Finally, the Michoud project manager responded, "That's not going to happen. There will be no failures on this program." I guess that was the last thing he wanted to hear. But I knew the reality of potentially using faulty materials or issues with the curing process that could cause defects. I remained quiet for the rest of the meeting.

Materials certification testing on the first composite nose cone several months later indicated it would not be able to withstand the high air flow and temperature extremes during ascent. It would lose its integrity and break apart, causing catastrophic debris to hit the Orbiter. The very first nose cone was unusable! A different layup and cure process was required to ensure that the nose cone would have permeability to allow retention of pressure buildup during high air flow and elevated temperature phases during flight.

Composite nose cone lay-up process

Composite nose cone preparing to be cured in the autoclave

In 1997, the first MSFC manufactured composite nose cone, ultimately thirteen pounds lighter than the metal one, was shipped to Michoud and certified flight-ready. It was installed atop ET-88 and led the way to space on the successful STS-86 mission.

Because the nose cones were entirely black and all looked identical, it was difficult to differentiate one from another. Early on in the program, the Composite Lab started an informal, in-house technique of nicknaming each nose cone. Of course, each one had an official serial number, but who wanted to rattle off all those numbers? It was much easier to go by the nicknames when informally communicating the production status of each nose cone. Everyone on the team was afforded the opportunity to proffer up a name for consideration and have it placed in the pipeline. Nicknames were usually after children, grandchildren, wives, and pets. The first nickname was Baby, followed by Daisy, Lucky, and Ginger, to name a few.

I believe that personalizing each nose cone was a constant reminder to us of what was at stake working in human space flight, and it pushed us to give each nose cone our 110 percent effort affording us our two minutes of fame!

Composite nose cone installed on External Tank

Woodism

Using things of the past can guide you to the future.

Requited Love

It's ironic how life can be so full yet, at the same time, so empty. My life was good. I had challenging, satisfying work, and my creative juices flowed through my woodworking and music. I was active in my church and had been a volunteer, operating the camera for taped television broadcast, for more than ten years. I owned my own home. Still, something was missing. I loved my independence, but at times, I was lonely. I was approaching my mid-thirties and was still single. I hadn't anticipated traveling through life alone. I remember saying to myself, "Scott, if you're going to meet someone, you have to make yourself available." But where to start?

I had fallen into the habit of turning down most social invitations. There just didn't seem to be enough hours in the day, and relationships, with their unknown complexities, represented a huge investment in time and commitment. But I finally reached a point where at least I was open to possibility. One night, a family friend, Bill, asked me, "Are you dating anyone?"

"I'm too busy to date seriously," I answered. "That may never happen." After this conversation, I became the subject of a covert matchmaking operation conceived and executed by my friends and family, specifically Bill and my mother.

In the late summer of 1993, my parents' church was planning its annual picnic, and Mom and Dad encouraged me to attend. Normally, I would have said no, but I was trying to be more open. Plus, Mom knew me well enough to invite me for the food rather than to meet an eligible female. I arrived late, after everyone had already finished eating, but thankfully, there was still plenty of food left. As I was finishing a cheeseburger, Bill introduced me to a friend, Dianne. The singles were gathering for a volleyball game, and she invited me to be on her team. I had always been drawn to brunettes, and I liked her long curly hair and petite, athletic frame. I sensed a gentleness about her.

Unfortunately, the day ended without my saying good-bye to her. Sometime after the volleyball game, I was talked into going on a "short" hike with the youth group, which, to my consternation, lasted much longer than anticipated. As I had feared, Dianne was gone by the time we returned. However, before she left, Mom invited her to join us for the white-water rafting trip the church had planned for the following weekend, and she accepted. Dianne had piqued my interest and I was intrigued. During the following week, I was up to my eyeballs in work, at both Lockheed Martin and the family business, and knowing I would see her on the weekend provided a nice distraction. This time, I would stay focused on her.

When Saturday finally rolled around, Dianne was at the church parking lot waiting for us. She had been expecting my mother to be part of the group, and when only the Phillips men showed up, the plan to get the two of us together became apparent. We went in one car, with Dianne and I sharing the backseat for the three-hour drive to the Ocoee River in Tennessee. We talked mostly about our jobs, and because Dianne was in human resources management and had earlier worked on the Space Shuttle Program, we had a lot to say. I was so absorbed in the conversation that the trip just flew by. As always, Steve enjoyed teasing me and couldn't resist asking about a girl I had once dated. I quickly changed the subject. Dad remained pretty quiet, no doubt enjoying our spirited exchange.

At the Ocoee, we parked at the bottom of the river and boarded a rickety, 1960s-era bus loaded with rafts and kayaks for the steep, bumpy ride to our starting point. Dianne got on first and I thought, *Oh no! She's sitting on the wrong side. I won't be able to hear her.* She wasn't aware that I was deaf in one ear, and I didn't want that to be one of the first things she learned about me. As it turned out, it served as the perfect excuse to lean in closer to her.

I felt a kindred spirit. I was drawn to her honesty and vulnerability as she shared details of her life. Through colleagues at work, I already knew some of her story, although I didn't know that she was the person they had been discussing until that day. Her husband had also worked on the Shuttle Program, but a couple of years earlier, he had committed suicide, leaving Dianne with her three stepdaughters aged eight, ten, and eighteen. She loved the girls and had put her heart and soul into raising them for five years. She fought to keep them, but after a difficult court battle, they moved back with their biological mother out of state. Practically overnight, Dianne went from having a family of five to being alone. Six months later, she suffered another blow with the unexpected death of her older sister. She shared with me about her journey of healing and her renewed faith. I was both impressed and captivated.

The bus trip was magical in a way. It was very early in our friendship, but I knew I wanted to spend more time with Dianne. For the first time in my life, I seriously wanted to continue further down that road. I hoped that she did too.

When we reached our destination, we were issued safety gear. When I saw Dianne struggling with her helmet, I was happy to come to her aid. The four of us plus two other people and a guide loaded into the raft and eagerly pushed off. The rapids were a Class 4, meaning a medium skill level was required. I felt protective of Dianne, but it was my first experience rafting, and I was somewhat apprehensive about my own well-being. Fortunately, we had a seasoned guide who instructed us on how to maneuver a 360-degree turn while flying through the rapids. The hour-long ride was exhilarating, to say the least, and part of the excitement for me was Dianne and I holding on to each other in the rough waters to keep from falling out. At the conclusion of the ride, we spent the next hour floating in our lifejackets the rest of the way to the parking lot.

Rafting down the Ocoee River in Tennessee

After a quick change of clothes, we returned our gear and started the drive home, which included a barbecue dinner on the way. Steve playfully harassed me by opening the back door of the car, pretending he was positioning himself in the backseat with Dianne. He was lucky to receive merely a shove! He smiled and gave me a thumbs-up.

Our first bona fide date was a day trip to my old stomping grounds in Florence for sightseeing and dinner. I wanted to share with her some of my first experiences in Alabama. We drove by our old house, my high school and, of course, the cemetery where I worked during the summers, which provided a perfect opportunity to share stories of my teenage shenanigans. We also visited Wilson Dam. As I framed her through my camera lens in front of the locks, I thought, *I'm looking at the real thing. I can see this woman possibly being my wife someday.* Fortunately, I had not been jaded by past hurts and still believed in love at first sight.

Dianne standing in front of Wilson Dam

Dianne had a sidekick and trusted companion: Astro, a Scottish terrier named after a science experiment from her tenure at the Space Shuttle Program. I knew I would have to win him over to get to Dianne. Whether we were at her home or mine, we would always walk Astro in the evenings, affording us lots of time to talk and get to know each other on a deeper level. I knew we were getting serious the day she commented on my décor: "Do you realize your house is decorated Early American Space Shuttle? You have 21 Shuttle items in your living room!"

"No way!" I said. "That's not possible!" I proceeded to count the models, bookends, lamps, pictures, and posters. I totaled 20.

"Don't forget the pencil sharpener!" she said. She was right: 21!

To my family's shock, I soon informed them that Dianne was The One. Mom asked, "Are you sure? You've known her only a couple of months." Most decisions in my life had been made based on intuition, and this was no exception. Dianne is intuitive as well, and we saw our lives coming together. My family was encouraged by our obvious happiness. We were at her house one evening talking about "what ifs," and I just popped the question. It seemed so natural at that moment to ask her to marry me. Fortunately, she said yes.

Later, I was touched when Dianne shared her journal with me. She had suffered so much, but was open to trusting again. Her trust made it easier for me to commit. There was a beautiful simplicity about our engagement, and we shared our happiness with friends and family—although I almost blew it the time I got distracted with work and my woodworking and failed to call her for several days. This was before we all became hardwired to cell phones. It wasn't very smart of me, though, and I vowed never to do that again.

Relaxing with friends during a hike in Tennessee

Dianne's late husband had been cremated, and she wanted to return his ashes to his parents in South Carolina before we were married. I supported her decision and offered to make the trip with her. I was a bit apprehensive, but his parents were very gracious. Dianne's stepdaughters lived nearby with their mother, and we took the opportunity to spend a couple of days together in Hilton Head so I could get to know them.

It was also very important to me that I meet Dianne's parents before we got married; so in November 1993, we drove 600 miles through a snowstorm to her hometown just outside of Detroit, Michigan. The long trip allowed us to spend an extended amount of time together, and the more I learned about her, the more deeply in love I fell.

Her father, Byron "Ty" Cobb, was a WWII veteran who had been the tail gunner on a B-25 Mitchell aircraft serving in the South Pacific. He told me he had made sure to do well on written tests because he preferred to serve in the air. He struck me as a fun-loving guy with a keen sense of humor, always ready with a joke to tell. When he first met me and saw my beard, he told Dianne, "I hope he doesn't own a motorcycle." Thankfully, I didn't—it may have been a deal-breaker! Her mother was gracious and kind, a dedicated wife and mother, and she also had great humor. It was obvious that Dianne's parents shared a deep love for one another, and I was touched by their devotion. As we were getting ready to return to Alabama, her mom said to me, "You fit in like an old shoe." It's true that when you marry, you marry the whole family. I've grown to love her entire family—in-laws and outlaws—as my own.

We were married on February 12, 1994, during a freak ice storm. It probably wasn't the most ideal month to pick for a wedding, and I have to take the credit. Dianne let me pick the date, and I thought it made sense to get married on my birthday so I'd never forget our anniversary. Oh, yeah! We could also throw in Valentine's Day along with it. Our parents and extended family members met for the first time at the wedding and became immediate friends. Most of our guests traveled from Ohio and Michigan, where they lived only about 100 miles apart. I thought, *Wouldn't you know it? I had to move south to meet a Northern girl!*

I was honored to have Steve as my best man, as I had been at his. My father and Bill served as my groomsmen. Dianne's sister, Cheryl, was her maid-of-honor and nieces, Ashley and Tiffiney were flower girls. As I watched Dianne walk down the aisle, I felt like the luckiest guy on the planet. I had found my soul mate. A couple of coworkers had remarked, "I came to your wedding, Phillips, just to see you actually get married!" At times, I, too, was skeptical that I would find the right person.

Mr. and Mrs. Scott Phillips. Courtesy Dennis Keim

For our honeymoon, we flew to Fort Myers, Florida, drove twenty miles up the coast to Port Charlotte, and took a twenty-minute boat ride to Palm Island. Cars are not allowed on the island, and we spent a quiet honeymoon walking along the two-mile stretch of pristine beach and enjoying our time together. And I think our friends and family eventually forgave us for having to drive through an ice storm to get to our wedding!

Dianne and Scott with their parents, Byron "Ty" and Lois Cobb and Dick and Mary Lue Phillips. Courtesy Dennis Keim

I had found the missing piece in my life. My life was full, and now, I had someone to share it with. And with the success of my parents' business, it was a perfect time to transfer my duties to the growing staff. We quickly took a big step forward into our life together. Dianne owned a home in Huntsville, and I had a house about thirty miles west of the city. We decided that we would sell both of our houses and combine our resources to build a new home. We worked well together on this project, and after a month or so of research, we agreed on a floor plan and a piece of property close to my home. While the house was being built, we initially lived in Dianne's home. When it sold four months later, we moved to my home. I think Dianne was relieved when it, too, sold four months later. I guess she had had enough of my over-the-top Space Shuttle décor. We experienced a smooth build, mainly due to our experienced general contractor, and our new home was ready to move into that September. Our combined furniture blended well, and fortunately, I wasn't forced to leave behind very much from my bachelor days. I still preferred my Space Shuttle memorabilia, but I let Dianne do the decorating.

And that was fine with me because I was busy setting up my new workshop in our extra garage bay.

Shortly before our wedding, I learned that my director of twelve years, Tony Andreoni, who was retiring, had nominated me to be the Launch Honoree for STS-62. As part of the Manned Space Flight Awareness Program, this award is presented to employees for their dedication to quality work and flight safety. The highly effective incentive program was developed under Werhner Von Braun as a way to remind manned space flight workers about importance of their work and the need for individual efforts to ensure the safety of the astronauts whose lives depended on the integrity of the hardware. It is the highest tribute paid by NASA and includes a one-week, all-expenses-paid trip for two to Kennedy Space Center as NASA VIPs. Honorees view a launch, tour the facilities, attend a reception in their honor, and meet with members of the Astronaut Corps and NASA officials. After committee review, I was selected for the honor.

The timing of the trip was perfect as Dianne and I were able to make it a highlight of our honeymoon. This was Dianne's second launch; I had been to many, but this was the first time as Launch Honoree! At the opening reception, we were warmly greeted by astronauts Jan Davis, Bob Crippen, Lauren Schriver, Brian Duffy, Cady Coleman, and Carl Waltz. The accommodations were superb, including a fully stocked hospitality room on our floor.

They planned a dinner one evening for the honorees and astronauts. The theme was Tacky Tourist Costume Party. Wearing plaid shorts and red suspenders, I managed to take third place. I don't think the astronauts were eligible to place, but if they had been, I would have voted, hands down, for Carl Waltz, who confidently walked into the room with a blow-up life preserver around his middle—in the shape of a duck!

Launch Honoree Reception with Astronaut
Bob Crippen. Courtesy NASA

Posing with Astronaut Brian Duffy at costume party. Courtesy NASA

Manned Flight Awareness Honoree Award with MSFC
Director, Porter Bridwell. Courtesy NASA

The weather cooperated all week and we were honored to
stand with the other VIPs across the Banana Creek to witness
the successful launch of STS-62.

Launch of STS-62

The year had started out with a bang, and I had found my groove...or so I thought.

Woodism

A house is simply a roof with four walls.
It becomes a home when you add love.

Line in the Sand

I returned from Kennedy Space Center to a new director, one with a very different management style. Our former director, Tony Andreoni, had promoted a positive work culture, and we were accustomed to high team spirit built on respect, trust, and mutual support for one another. We were used to inclusiveness and camaraderie. Tony saw the importance of scheduling such events as picnics and holiday parties not only for the employees but also for their spouses and children. He knew that strong support at home translated into dedicated workers and thus promoted the overall success of our mission.

Annual Martin Marietta Family Picnic at MSFC

Tony helped establish the Productivity Enhancement Complex to house in one building all prime contractors performing research and development on External Tank, Solid Rocket Boosters, and Main Engines for the Shuttle Program. Equipment, tools, and expertise were shared and communication with NASA was streamlined. My division, the R&D arm of the NASA External Tank Projects Office, was a family of 150 highly skilled people encompassing logistics, finance, contracts, information technology, planning, tool design, safety, quality, and engineers and technicians working in welding, foam, and composites.

Productivity Enhancement Complex at MSFC

My first exposure to the new management style we were under was during staff meetings, where I would repeatedly hear the question, "How was it done before?" After my explanation, I would receive the automatic reply, "Well, we're not doing it that way anymore." I sensed our new director was drawing a line in the sand. We were rapidly transitioning to an autocratic mind-set that was ushering in fear and apprehension—and a closed-door policy. Over the next six months, our team—many of whom had been in their jobs for at least fifteen years—struggled with constantly changing procedures, micromanagement, and petty retributions. Family functions became a memory and morale took a nosedive.

One day in October 1994, I received an urgent schedule request late in the day to ship one gallon of specially blended External Tank primer from Huntsville to our Michoud facility in New Orleans overnight. The primer was a flammable material, which meant following stringent shipping procedures. Because commercial carriers of hazardous material require mountains of paperwork and have numerous hoops to jump through, such as using specialized packaging, labeling, and documentation, it normally required more than a one-day turnaround. Our team in New Orleans would face a potential work stoppage without the critical material.

Fortunately, my logistics counterpart from New Orleans, Mike McCann, whom I had worked closely with for almost ten years, was in Huntsville for a meeting and was scheduled to drive back that evening. He was in my office when I received the urgent call and volunteered to hand-carry the material to the receiving dock at Michoud as a way to expedite the shipment—a process we had used many times. In logistics, our goal was always to be as responsive as possible, and it was important for Huntsville to be able to meet this requirement. I briefed my local quality manager, and he verbally sanctioned the hand-carry. Normally, I would have secured his signature on the shipping document, but by the time I finished the paperwork, he had already left for the day. And since we had handled rush situations like this in the past, he obviously wasn't concerned about signing the paperwork either. I attached the shipper to the can of primer and safely secured it in Mike's vehicle for the six-hour drive to New Orleans.

What I didn't know was that there had been some previous issues within the External Tank Program at Michoud; specifically, site audits had turned up incomplete documentation for hazardous material shipments. This triggered NASA to inform our management that the next time there was an infraction involving hazardous materials, they were to punish the individuals involved. The primer arrived in New Orleans ahead of schedule. A member of our Huntsville team—a manager who thrived on stirring things up and causing chaos as a way of maintaining control—was on the loading dock and noticed that there wasn't a signature on the shipping documentation. He contacted our new director and reminded him of the edict from NASA. I was stunned that one of our own guys would feel compelled to report such an insignificant incident, which could potentially affect our award fee from NASA. It reminded me of a scene from *The Andy Griffith Show* with Gomer Pyle conducting a citizen's arrest.

We worked hundreds of quality issues together for more than ten years—many with only a verbal okay—so I assumed that the quality manager would confirm that he had given a verbal authorization. I was called into the director's office to tell my side of the story. When the quality guy was called in and asked if he had approved the shipment, he told a bold-faced lie that he had not. I was stunned. I realized the days of coworkers covering each other's backs were over. It was now every man for himself.

The situation was blown totally out of proportion. As far as safety was concerned, that can of primer was no more dangerous than a can of lighter fluid from Home Depot. The company spent thousands of dollars and well over a month investigating the circumstances surrounding the incident. A Martin Marietta Internal Affairs representative was sent to Huntsville to interview the people involved. They reviewed our policies and practices and poured over every piece of documentation. Throughout the investigation, our quality manager continued to say that he had not given authorization, and management was all too eager to acquiesce to the NASA directive. Even though I had no previous infractions on my record, I was forced to endure, throughout the entire investigation, the threat of possibly losing my job. They decided to make an example out of me. My punishment was a thirty-day leave without pay.

The quality and integrity of my work was well-known throughout our team and the Shuttle Program. My work was highly respected and people across the country depended on my knowledge and expertise. Without exception—from workers to the top echelon—everyone considered the punishment excessive and unjustified. My colleagues would call me at home, saying, "This is stupid and crazy. Nothing is getting done at work." They were rattled knowing they could be next. Many of them decided to boycott the annual Christmas party that year and came to my home instead to show their solidarity.

About two weeks into my leave, a Martin Marietta vice president who respected my work and trusted my honesty and integrity in this situation intervened. He apologized that I had been the one to take the fall, and I was back on the job the next day. But to add insult to injury, when I arrived back at work, to my shock and disbelief, I was informed that I would be reporting to a new manager, the very person who had started the fiasco— "Gomer Pyle"! I was further notified that I would be facing a mandatory departmental audit later that week. I didn't know whether or not that had factored into my early return, but I made sure I passed the audit with 100 percent.

To top it all off, I was flabbergasted to learn that, while I was on leave, we had received the unused hazardous material back from New Orleans in the same container—without the proper signatures on the paperwork. And the kicker: My new manager chose not to challenge it. No investigation was ever performed. Through it all, had it not been for my strong dedication to the program and the support of my family and coworkers, I am sure I would have succumbed to my own "Auggie Dog" moment.

Two years after the paint incident, I was at a conference with the quality manager who had "approved" the shipment. I said to him, "You realize you lied." He turned red and said, "Let's move on and get over it." I felt vindicated. Clearly, he knew it had happened just as I had said.

Unfortunately, my punishment didn't end with my return to work. As a direct result of the incident, I was passed over on the next two annual pay raises, which translated to a substantial financial loss by the end of my career. Additionally, I had to endure more than two years of monthly mandatory safety meetings in which I was subtly reminded in front of my peers that I would not be receiving any awards.

I had an epiphany of sorts as I came to realize I could be sold out in a flash. Until that point, our team had always been able to rely on a person's word, and I had a strong allegiance toward my management.

Even though my role was small, my vision was large and my enthusiasm and dedication for the program never wavered. I continued to go the extra mile for my colleagues and customers. However, my interactions with my management were always guarded and often contentious.

Management admonished our team from fraternizing with NASA personnel at receptions and outside activities over concerns of potential conflicts of interest. Even when we were invited to attend official Manned Space Flight Awareness events such as astronaut crew debriefings and no conflict of interest existed, the directive stood. There were no exceptions.

I was already well connected and thoroughly vetted throughout NASA in terms of both my professional work and my artwork. NASA Public Affairs was beginning to understand my vision and appreciated what I was trying to achieve in sharing my enthusiasm for the program and documenting the Shuttle Program through my collections and artwork. In fact, several NASA project offices had commissioned my Shuttle models for employees who were retiring or transferring to other locations. I was carrying the legacy to future generations. Because part of my vision included having astronauts sign my artwork and memorabilia, I wasn't going to be discouraged from attending events where I could meet them. I would have to draw my own line in the sand. Almost everyone else on my team toed the line with the overregulated mind-set, but I continued to network and attend astronaut events and special ceremonies, although I made sure I did it within the framework of NASA protocol.

Post STS-117 debrief at MSFC. Courtesy NASA

Post STS-120 debrief with Astronaut
Stephanie Wilson. Courtesy NASA

Post ISS Expedition 4 debrief with astronauts, Carl
Waltz and Captain Dan Bursch. Courtesy NASA

Post STS-121 debrief with astronauts (l. to r.) Lisa Nowak, Steve Lindsey (Commander), and Mark Kelly. Courtesy NASA

Post STS-122 debrief. Courtesy NASA

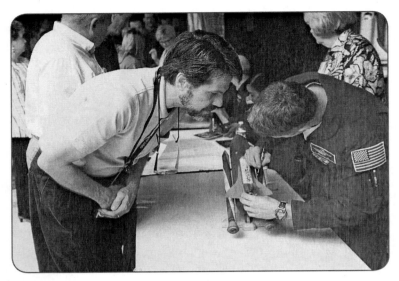

Post STS-131 debrief with James Dutton (pilot). Courtesy NASA

Post STS-129 debrief with crew members. Courtesy NASA

Often getting into these events required some creativity on my part. I either coordinated my schedule to make sure I was at the right place at the right time or I took vacation to support my endeavors. Even though there were often long periods between events when I would have to stay focused and motivated, I found these interactions to be empowering, participating in them provided me a sense of accomplishment and moved me forward in achieving my goal of documenting firsthand stories. I knew the potential risks by taking this path, but my desire to preserve and document the Shuttle Program in this unique way was a driving force.

It was strictly against the Code of Federal Regulations (CFR) for NASA to show favoritism to a contractor or to interfere in their internal affairs. However, my position in logistics and the interest in my one-of-a-kind artwork afforded me myriad opportunities to develop close working relationships with NASA personnel and its top echelon. It was not standard protocol for a contractor to be in the NASA Shuttle Projects Office, but a year or so after the absurd paint incident, they called me into their office. "We want you to know the edict came out of our office," they said. "There was nothing malicious toward you. We are sorry it happened to you." They reassured me that NASA had full confidence in my work and in my integrity. I needed to hear that from my customer.

Throughout the ordeal, it would have been so easy to be consumed with anger and bitterness, but my passion sustained me and allowed me to move forward and maintain my enthusiasm while pursuing my lifelong journey of continuing the legacy of the Shuttle Program.

Woodism

The nail that sticks out the furthest is the one that gets hit the hardest.

Danger on the High Seas

My work in logistics required knowledge of all types of transportation, including maritime rules and regulations. During my suspension, I continued to receive status updates from my transportation team at Michoud, and I learned of a serious situation unfolding that could potentially embarrass NASA and cause a major delay to an already tight schedule of the Space Shuttle Program. This is a little-known story involving an amazing rescue mission, filled with heroism and danger on the high seas.

On November 10, 1994, ET-70 was loaded on a NASA-owned barge, heading for Kennedy Space Center. The tank was slated for the hundredth "manned" mission and would propel Atlantis to its first visit to the Russian space station, Mir. The *Poseidon*—a 265-foot, unmanned, 40-year-old, WWII, covered barge that had been modified during the Saturn program—was being towed by a tug with a crew of five led by Captain Lanny Wiles. The well-seasoned, 114-foot *Orgeron*, with twin engines totaling 3500 horsepower, was towing the External Tank the 900 miles from Michoud to KSC, normally a five-day journey. Shortly after leaving Michoud with the $53-million payload, *Orgeron*'s jokey bar, which connected its two rudders, broke, resulting in a complete disabling of the starboard rudder. The *Orgeron* chose not to return for repairs and pressed on, relying on the port rudder to see them through.

On November 13, as the *Orgeron* and its tow started to round the southern tip of Florida, they began receiving weather reports of heavy winds and strong seas generated by Tropical Storm Gordon. Concerned by the rapidly deteriorating conditions, Captain Wiles, with twenty years of experience at sea, radioed his company, Montco, asking to seek shelter from the storm in Miami. Permission was denied. NASA requested them to continue on.

On the night of November 14, the *Orgeron* began to lose power. Because of the severity of the storm and the back and forth rocking of the tug, sediment inside the fuel tanks loosened and began to clog the filters entering the engine. Because of the 2,500 gallons of fuel required daily, the onboard engineer, who was young and inexperienced, was unable to keep the fuel lines cleared. First, one engine went out completely, and then the second lost partial power. The tug continued to make slow progress along the Florida coast, but by late evening, it had lost all engine power due to the fuel contamination. At the time, the *Orgeron* and the *Poseidon* were eight to ten miles off the coast of Florida between Fort Pierce and Kennedy Space Center.

The storm was in full force, with blinding rain and seas breaking eighteen to twenty feet high. Without engine power, *Orgeron* and the barge carrying ET-70 were left adrift. The barge began to be blown toward shore, aided by the sail effect of *Poseidon*'s tall, Quonset-hut-style cover, carrying the latched down ET-70 on its transporter. Captain Wiles knew his tug and crew were in grave danger and notified the Coast Guard. But because of the storm's ferocity, the Coast Guard was unable to help. Wiles considered that it might be necessary to release the barge with the External Tank and allow it to meet its disastrous fate.

As a last ditch effort, the Coast Guard radioed all nearby ships stating that, if possible, any assistance rendered would be appreciated. The request was picked up by the *Cherry Valley*, a steam-powered, 688-foot, single-hull oil tanker headed toward Jacksonville with a crew of 25. This $7.5-million vessel, built in 1974, was laden with 9 million gallons of heavy fuel oil and required a 35-foot draft. Under no obligation to assist and unaware of the cargo being towed, Captain Skip Strong immediately altered course to rendezvous with the tug, steering his very cumbersome vessel toward perilous shoal waters. He arrived on the scene several hours after the *Orgeron* had lost power.

In a normal tow, 2,000-foot lines are used, but because the *Cherry Valley* was not typically used for towing, the plan was to pass her heavily worn, 9-inch diameter, 700-foot-long mooring lines to the tug to keep it from moving toward the rocky shoals, which would likely destroy both the vessel and the barge holding the External Tank. The first pass came up short, as did the second. With water conditions becoming increasingly treacherous, Captain Strong decided to try one more time. He skillfully steered the Cherry Valley even closer, despite the torrential downpour and low visibility. With the help of onboard radar and *Orgeron*'s generators providing running lights, his persistence paid off. Under extremely dangerous conditions, with the vessels close enough to scrape paint off their sides, the seamen handed over the mooring lines and joined the vessels together.

Strong radioed Wiles and asked, "Now that we have things settled down a bit, what the hell do we have on the barge?" Wiles responded, "I didn't want to tell you before, but it's the liquid fuel cell for the Space Shuttle." Before Strong could ask, "Is it explosive?" Wiles assured him that the fuel cell was inert. The two men then agreed on three possible scenarios, based on sea and weather conditions, to move forward: continue with the tug and barge in tow, drop the barge and take only the tug, or rescue the crew and let go of both the tug and barge.

The vessels were now less than one mile from the shoals and approaching shallow water. At this point, Captain Strong was fearful of running aground and causing a potentially catastrophic oil spill. *Cherry Valley's* 90,000-pound, 22-1/2-foot copper propeller was churning up mud, indicating it had neared the bottom. With the tug and *Poseidon* in tow, the oil tanker steamed slowly in a southeasterly direction while the crew members of *Cherry Valley* wrapped the ends of the lines in canvas. For the better part of a day, they vigilantly greased the lines to avoid chaffing due the violent pitch and yaw of the vessels and the potential snapping of the lines—much like a rubber band—which could possibly injure or kill the deck crew with recoil. Captain Strong called his company, Margate/Keystone Shipping, to let them know they had successfully saved the crew and that he they were towing an External Tank for the Space Shuttle Program. After a long pause on the other end, his company communicated support but expressed concerns for the environment. Strong responded, "I have a sharpened fire axe on deck to cut loose if we are in jeopardy."

Another tug, *South Bend*, out of Fort Pierce, was monitoring the Coast Guard's channel and attempted to assist in completing the tow. Because of violent squalls, the *South Bend* was overwhelmed and underpowered. While retreating, the tug took on so much water that the captain had to run it aground to avoid sinking. The Coast Guard later delivered pumps, and the *South Bend* returned safely to port.

With weather conditions worsening and the chance of overstressing the mooring lines, as well as the intricacy of maintaining their position to steer into the wind serving as a break for the flotilla, Captain Strong decided it was best to anchor and ride out the rest of the storm. All night and the following day, the *Cherry Valley* with the *Orgeron* and *Poseidon* in tow stayed anchored, maintaining and replacing lines as needed.

Two nine-inch-diameter mooring lines secured between the J. A. Orgeron and the Cherry Valley. Courtesy Captain Skip Strong

On the evening of November 16, NASA dispatched two much newer tugs, the robust *Dorothy Moran* out of Jacksonville and the *Ocean Wind* out of Fort Pierce, to relieve the *Cherry Valley* of the tow. As with the *South Bend*, the *Dorothy Moran* failed on her first attempt and was forced to retreat. *Cherry Valley* hunkered down another day with the flotilla. By this time, the crew had worked courageously around the clock for two tense days. When the storm finally ebbed, the *Dorothy Moran*, accompanied by the Michoud harbor master who originally loaded the tank, arrived.

While on the bridge preparing to release the flotilla, Captain Strong received an unexpected satellite call from a company representative and its lawyer. They congratulated him on the successful rescue and then went on to describe a salvage rule entitling the company to receive a fee for saving the External Tank. *Cherry Valley's* lawyer felt they had a strong case since the salvage was successful, and there was concern that the *Dorothy Moran* might lay claim. He was instructed not to release the flotilla until *Cherry Valley* received a signed credit for salvage.

Captain Strong was eager to relieve his ship and crew, and he felt his authority was being usurped by having to wait an unspecified time. With consternation and despite the risk to his job, he gave an ultimatum, allowing them thirty minutes to secure the paperwork before he released the barge to the *Dorothy Moran* to finish the job. He reluctantly instructed the tugs to stand down. Exactly thirty minutes later, he received the call confirming receipt of the signed document. Following a well-choreographed and skillful transfer of lines from the *Orgeron*, Strong released the barge to the *Dorothy Moran*, and the *Poseidon* was successfully towed the rest of the distance to the Kennedy Space Center. The disabled *Orgeron* was then transferred to the *Ocean Wind* and towed back to Fort Pierce for major repairs. Upon arrival at Kennedy Space Center, the External Tank was inspected and found to be surprisingly unharmed from the ordeal.

Successful transfer of the Orgeron and Poseidon from
the Cherry Valley. Courtesy Captain Skip Strong

It is standard procedure for each External Tank to be accompanied by a Department of Defense document (DD250) that contains the estimated production cost of the tank. The cost of ET-70 was $53,803,000. The legal team of the *Cherry Valley*'s owner, Margate/Keystone Shipping, stepped in to claim a percentage of the value for rescuing the tank.

I have always been intrigued by maritime law and, during my career in logistics, became a student of the subject. In researching the history of salvage awards, I discovered that modern awards are based on an incident in the San Francisco harbor back in 1867 involving a 1200-ton British ship, the *Blackwall*, which was anchored in the harbor when 38,000 sacks of wheat suddenly caught fire. When the crew failed to douse the blaze, they sent a verbal alarm and the nearby fire department sprang into action. The fire department, however, was without a fire boat and convinced the crew of a steam tug, *Goliath*, moored at the dock, to allow them to load water pumping units onto its ship. The *Goliath* approached the burning ship, which was almost totally ablaze by this point, and most of the crew had abandoned ship by lifeboats. The captain of the *Goliath*, carrying the fire equipment, came alongside the *Blackwall*, allowing firemen to board and extinguish the flames. The ship and cargo were valued at $100,000. The owner of the *Goliath* filed a salvage claim, which went all the way to the Supreme Court. The findings were that without the use of the *Goliath* to carry the fire equipment, the *Blackwall*, crew, and cargo would have been killed or destroyed. The foundation of a salvage claim was based on the considerable skill necessary to bring in a ship to help, despite risks to ship and crew. Today, we have what is known as Blackwall Factors:

1. Labor expended by salvers in rendering help,
2. Skill and energy displayed in rendering service and saving the property,
3. Value of property employed by the salvers in rendering the service and the danger to which such property was exposed,

4. Risk incurred by salvers in securing property from impending peril,
5. Value of the property saved,
6. Degree of danger from which the property was rescued, and
7. Skill and effort of salvers in preventing or minimizing damage to the environment (This point was added after the Exxon Valdez accident).

These points were applied to the value of saving the External Tank when a battle in the courts began one year later. Department of Justice Associate Attorney General Frank Hunger (brother-in-law of then-vice president Al Gore) was appalled by the out-of-court settlement proffered by his subordinates of $5 million. He initially countered with $1 million, which he felt was ample for two and half days of work. This forced Margate/Keystone Shipping to continue litigation in the District Court of Louisiana to achieve a percentage of the value of the External Tank and the barge. The judge in the case determined the External Tank was specialized property without market value and appraised it at replacement cost.

NASA External Tank Program managers from MSFC, Craig Sumner and Jody (Adams) Singer, testified that ET-70, if lost, would have been replaced with ET-71, which was DD250 valued at $51.4 million. It was revealed that current NASA accounting procedures allowed $50 million per year to maintain a sustained assembly line of four tanks (approximately $12 million per tank) at all times as an insurance policy for any lost, damaged, or unusable tanks. It was also discovered that just six months prior to this incident, Lockheed Martin (formerly Martin Marietta) had offered NASA an option of four tanks at $19 million each and allowing for increased lead time. This plan would avoid the extra cost of round-the-clock shifts and overtime pay. NASA rejected the offer because they already had four tanks in circulation and a system in place to pay a premium for flight ready tanks.

Margate/Keystone Shipping, headed by top lawyers from around the country, pursued the claim in Louisiana. The District Court recognized the ET-71 replacement cost of $51.4 million plus the $2 million *Poseidon* replacement value at 12.5 percent, based on Blackwall Factors. The percentage also took into consideration the severity of the storm and the fact that no crew or vessels were lost. The award could have been as high as 25 percent. At just over $6 million, this was the largest maritime pure salvage claim to date.

Frank Hunger, persistent in not wanting to pay this exorbitant amount out of the US Treasury, agreed to an increased out-of-court settlement of $3.3 million. Again, Margate/Keystone Shipping's legal team rejected the offer. One year later, the DOJ appealed to the Fifth Appellate District Court. The higher court agreed with the percentage and all points of the Blackwall Factors, except for No. 5 on the value of the property saved, saying the lower court erred by using the DD250 cost of the tank, which included research and development as well as overhead costs. The court determined that the actual replacement cost should have been used—Lockheed Martin's previous offer to NASA of $19 million per tank, and NASA's accounting practice to pay $12 million to maintain an open pipeline to produce each tank. The replacement value was determined to be $19 million, $12 million to keep the pipeline open, plus $2 million for the Poseidon—a total of $33 million. The final judgment awarded, with interest, was $4.7 million—within spitting distance of the original out-of-court settlement offered by the DOJ of $5 million—four years earlier. Still, it is the largest pure salvage settlement to-date with an award of $4,736,872, of which 63 percent went to Margate/Keystone and 37 percent was divided between the 25 crew members of the *Cherry Valley*.

I felt compelled to tell this little-known story of inspiration, risk-taking, and danger. As with my own journey, this is an example of what it took every day to achieve what was accomplished during the Space Shuttle Program. NASA was transporting a multi-million-dollar tank on a 40-year-old, modified WWII barge being towed by the lowest bidder. Captain Skip Strong was a graduate of the Naval Academy and just 32 years old when he made the heroic decision to rescue the *Orgeron* and the crew towing the *Poseidon*. I initially thought that his decision was out of national pride. I was impressed when I learned he had no idea what cargo the *Orgeron* was towing when he answered the call for help. It was about saving lives. His concern was that he knew he might find himself in a similar situation one day, and so he followed an unspoken maritime code to come to the rescue of a vessel in distress. Ironically, just two weeks after rescuing the *Orgeron*, he accidentally ran the *Cherry Valley* on a sandbar and had to radio for several tugs to pull him off.

The ET-70 trip was the first time Captain Lanny Wiles commanded a tow of this value. He continued to work for Montco as one of their top captains for the remainder of his career. His company was again contracted to tow the now-empty *Poseidon* back home to the Michoud facility—this time using a different tug.

Going forward, NASA modified their procedures. They built a new barge, *Pegasus*, which was fitted with upgraded anchors, and they ceased using tugs to tow the tanks from Michoud to Kennedy Space Center. Instead, they began employing the use of the solid rocket booster recovery ships to transport the barge.

At the launch of ET-70 on STS-71, commanded by Hoot Gibson, to Mir space station, some members of the crew of the *Cherry Valley* were in attendance. I was reminded of the raw human effort put forth by the seafaring crew to heroically save the tank. Here were two captains—with everything to lose—working together for a common goal of saving lives and valuable cargo. It further reinforced my belief that the Space Shuttle program was always about the human spirit—people who made the tough decisions and took the risks to achieve win-win results—like patriots Captain Skip Strong, Captain Lanny Wiles, and their valiant crews.

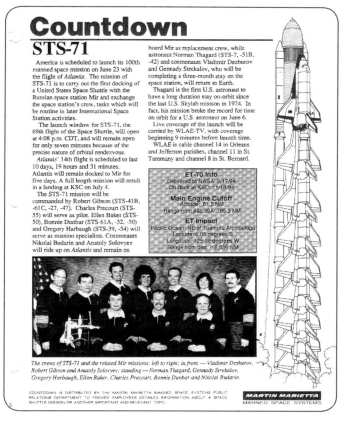

Countdown
STS-71

America is scheduled to launch its 100th manned space mission on June 23 with the flight of *Atlantis*. The mission of STS-71 is to carry out the first docking of a United States Space Shuttle with the Russian space station Mir and exchange the space station's crew, tasks which will be routine in later International Space Station activities.

The launch window for STS-71, the 69th flight of the Space Shuttle, will open at 4:08 p.m. CDT, and will remain open for only seven minutes because of the precise nature of orbital rendezvous.

Atlantis' 14th flight is scheduled to last 10 days, 19 hours and 31 minutes. Atlantis will remain docked to Mir for five days. A full length mission will result in a landing at KSC on July 4.

The STS-71 mission will be commanded by Robert Gibson (STS-41B, -61C, -27, -47). Charles Precourt (STS-55) will serve as pilot. Ellen Baker (STS-50), Bonnie Dunbar (STS-61A, -32, -50) and Gregory Harbaugh (STS-39, -54) will serve as mission specialists. Cosmonauts Nikolai Budarin and Anatoly Solovyev will ride up on *Atlantis* and remain on

board Mir as replacement crew, while astronaut Norman Thagard (STS-7, -51B, -42) and cosmonauts Vladimir Dezhurov and Gennady Strekalov, who will be completing a three-month stay on the space station, will return to Earth.

Thagard is the first U.S. astronaut to have a long duration stay on-orbit since the last U.S. Skylab mission in 1974. In fact, his mission broke the record for time on orbit for a U.S. astronaut on June 6.

Live coverage of the launch will be carried by WLAE-TV, with coverage beginning 9 minutes before launch time.

WLAE is cable channel 14 in Orleans and Jefferson parishes, channel 11 in St. Tammany and channel 8 in St. Bernard.

ET-70 Info
Delivered to NASA: 2/17/94
On dock at KSC: 11/18/94

Main Engine Cutoff
Altitude: 61.5 NM
Range from pad 39A: 785.3 NM

ET Impact
Pacific Ocean: NE of Tuamotu Archipelago
Latitude: 0.05 degrees S
Longitude: 125.38 degrees W
Range from pad: 6,836 NM

The crews of STS-71 and the related Mir missions: left to right; in front — Vladimir Dezhurov, Robert Gibson and Anatoly Solovyev; standing — Norman Thagard, Gennady Strekalov, Gregory Harbaugh, Ellen Baker, Charles Precourt, Bonnie Dunbar and Nikolai Budarin.

COUNTDOWN IS DISTRIBUTED BY THE MARTIN MARIETTA MANNED SPACE SYSTEMS PUBLIC RELATIONS DEPARTMENT TO PROVIDE EMPLOYEES DETAILED INFORMATION ABOUT A SPACE SHUTTLE MISSION OR ANOTHER IMPORTANT AND RELEVANT TOPIC.

MARTIN MARIETTA
MANNED SPACE SYSTEMS

The 100th "manned" space mission on STS-71 with Orbiter Atlantis

---

Woodism

*He who avoids risk has little to show
at the end of the day.*

Unconditional Love

I've learned that nothing is a given in life, not even life itself.
After an unexpected pregnancy and then suffering a miscarriage, Dianne was experiencing pain but was reassured that it was a result of the miscarriage. The intensity continued to increase, so much so that exploratory surgery was performed. We received the diagnosis that she had experienced an ectopic pregnancy, resulting in a rupture of her fallopian tube. More than 1,200 cubic centimeters of blood was pumped from her abdomen.

We had been excited about the pregnancy, but we were also realistic about our age and about the potential risks. I had waited so long to find Dianne, and now, after almost losing her, my apprehension grew with the fear of another pregnancy.

Up to that point, children were definitely not on my radar. As a child, I knew I was loved, but with the struggles of growing up in a large family, I had the predetermined mind-set that children were a burden, both financially and emotionally. I grew up believing there was a direct correlation between what I did and the love I received. I was content with not having children, but Dianne was not okay with that. On our long walks with Astro, we often discussed my deep-seated concerns. We had many intense, soul-searching conversations but I was not convinced. All I could think about was how long I had worked and how long I had waited to find the love of my life and how full our lives would be with vacations, sports cars, and self-absorbed frivolities. In spite of all of the good I had done in my life, I was selfish.

Our first of several cruises

Scott's selfie

As time passed, with another miscarriage and the clock ticking, Dianne began to talk about adoption. That was definitely not part of my plan. All I ever heard about adoption were heartbreaking stories about couples who prepared their lives and opened their hearts and their wallets only to see their dreams shattered when circumstances, beyond their control, changed. She mentioned adoption and I heard lawyers, fees, greed, competition, disappointment, and long agonizing waits. She wasn't even sure exactly how to navigate through the process or even where to begin. I listened as a way to validate and appease her, but I decided this was not going to happen. She calmly and lovingly told me she would continue to pray for wisdom and a softening of my heart.

Sometimes, one simple decision can set off a life-altering chain of events. One day, while driving home from work, I spotted an older gentleman on the side of the road trying to change his flat tire in the rain. I felt compelled to pull over to help and realized that I knew the man, a NASA colleague named Dick Holmes. As we changed the tire beneath an umbrella, we began to catch up on each other's lives. "I saw your wedding picture in the paper a few years ago," he said. "Any kids yet?" It was not a foregone conclusion that we would pursue adoption, but I gave him a half-hearted answer, "We're potentially looking into adoption." That seemed to pique his interest. As we parted, he thanked me profusely for my help, and as I walked back to my van, he called after me, "By the way, I have a friend at church who has an adoption ministry. I'll have him send you some information." I responded with a courteous "thank you" and blew it off without further thought.

A month or so later, after finishing some yard work one afternoon, I collected a stack of mail from the box and, without glancing through it, brought the bundle into the house for Dianne to sort through. She immediately spotted a large envelope. "Do you know anything about this package from Lifeline Children's

Services?" she asked. It dawned on me it was probably the organization Dick told me about. I told her about repairing the tire in the rain and that I hadn't mentioned it because I didn't expect to actually receive anything. Her face lit up when she started reading and realized that it was a Christian adoption agency. Inside was paperwork to start the adoption process. Requirements called for us to be married five years, which we were quickly approaching, and then to wait one additional year from the time of our initial application. I was face-to-face with my worst fears yet I allowed the process to continue. Without hesitation, Dianne completed the paperwork.

With the paperwork submitted, the wait began. Two weeks later, we received a call from the agency to schedule the initial interview. I was filled with apprehension—finances, our age, major change—but I reluctantly agreed to go. Dianne had been through so much, both physically and emotionally, and I hated to disappoint her. I rationalized, "The least I can do is go with an open mind. It doesn't mean that anything will come of it." A week later, we met with the director of the organization and he explained their ministry of helping and supporting young women who were experiencing a difficult and challenging time in their lives. I saw the love and the beauty that went into their ministry and the fact that the birth mothers were able to select the family spoke volumes to me. That day was a turning point for me. What I learned totally dispelled everything I thought I knew about adoption. For the first time, I could see the process without the drama and the agony, but it was still hard for me to visualize our life with a child. My fears were slowly subsiding, but I had strong doubts considering our age, and the thought of a long wait was daunting. We continued to be proactive and our follow-up interviews at the agency satisfied Dianne with the direction and focus she needed.

Exactly one year later, as promised, our home study began. Our social worker, Lynn, visited several times to evaluate our home life and interactions with each other and to get our responses to some serious questions. She was very kind and we felt very comfortable interacting with her. It was during this time and because of these questions that I examined my belief system around raising children and gradually came to terms with my misconceptions. It was no longer frightening to me. We prepared a twelve-page profile that included pictures, interests, and philosophical ideals. They checked out our finances, family members, and friends, and even conducted an FBI background check.

We completed the study in September 1999, and by November, only a few details remained before our profile could be presented to a potential birth mother. Lynn told us, "Now the hard part starts, waiting for an infant." We had been proactive and were confident we had done everything we could and resigned ourselves to go the distance. Our only concern was our ages. Would a birth mother select us, knowing that we were in our forties? We knew there were so many couples waiting, couples much younger than us.

One week later, a young woman presented at the emergency room in labor. She made the decision to choose adoption and requested a Christian organization. After a call to Lifeline and an assessment by a social worker, our profile was presented along with four others. Incredibly, the following week, Dianne received a call at work that we had a baby boy, born November 10. Instead of calling me on the phone, on her way home, she picked up a huge helium balloon, "It's a Boy," and had it waiting when I came home from work. I didn't get it at first, but she gave me time to process. When I finally understood what it meant, I was stunned and elated. I fell to my knees in disbelief. The reality hit me that I was actually going to become a father.

Our social worker later told us that at their weekly meeting, the staff at Lifeline saw similar likes and interests and decided to submit our profile even though all the details had not been finalized. "Other couples have waited longer," she said, "but we're also about matching families."

We named him Christian. His birth mother was only eighteen years old and a freshman in college. We were so grateful for the courage and loving decision she made in choosing to bring him into the world and allowing us the privilege of raising him. After so many trips to the adoption agency, this time we were finally bringing our child home. Seeing Christian for the first time was more powerful and emotional than I expected. He was perfect in every way with beautiful red hair. We carefully strapped him in his car seat and started our two-hour ride home. During the drive, I reflected on how ignorant I had been about adoption and how hard I had been on Dianne. At that moment, I knew I would be forever grateful for her patience, love, and understanding. She believed this moment would happen, and here we were, beginning our new adventure as parents.

Holding Christian for the first time

We adjusted easily into our parental roles and I embraced this new experience. I was eager to help decorate his room and enthusiastic to feed him, change diapers, or whatever was needed; I wanted to be a hands-on dad. We thanked God daily for bringing Christian into our lives. Our family and friends embraced our new family and their love and support meant so much to us. We came to realize that people made a connection between red hair and good fortune. We often joked that we should have charged every time someone asked to touch his hair for good luck!

Our redheaded gift–Christian Andrew Phillips

The adoption was "closed," meaning families would remain anonymous. However, when Christian was three months old, his biological mother contacted Lifeline to see if we would be willing to meet her at the adoption agency. We said, "Yes, absolutely!" We knew it was the right thing to do and that it would give us additional background information that we would not have otherwise had. Lynn joined us and we talked nonstop for over two hours. His birth mother was extremely bright, honest, and free-spirited. We loved her immediately for her heart as we already loved her for her brave decision.

Six months later, just when we were starting to feel in control, we received a call from the adoption agency that she was about to deliver a sibling for Christian, and she wanted to know if we would welcome the new baby into our family. It was an easy decision. We both squealed into the phone, "Absolutely!" We had prayed for one child, and God chose to doubly bless us! Our beautiful blond-haired, blue-eyed Tyler (named after his grandpa, Ty Cobb) was born on September 8, 2000, and we brought him home two days later. If we thought we were busy before—wow!— we had no idea! Diapers, and car seats and *Sesame Street* became our way of life.

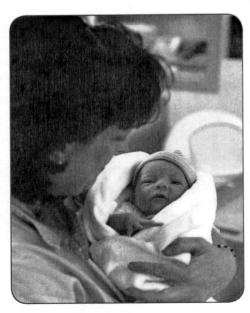

Picking up Tyler Alexander Phillips from the hospital

Working full-time became increasingly difficult for Dianne, and we knew that having someone else raise our children while we were away defeated the purpose of our mission of raising our boys. So she said good-bye to a job she loved, and to this day, she tells me, "I came home to an even better one." Going from two incomes to one was an additional challenge, one that we faced head on and never looked back.

Simple fun with Tyler and Christian

Our new family completely transformed our lives. Music was always a big part of my life and the overwhelming love I felt for my sons inspired me to play my guitar more and I began to write music. I wrote a song for Christian called "Christian Forever" and performed it at his christening. I was inspired to write Tyler's song one day after their evening bath. They thought it would be fun to add bubble bath to the Jacuzzi, which must have been most of the bottle, and it turned into a child's dream—an enormous bubble cave. While I was cleaning up the mess, I was inspired to write "Bubbles He Made."

Playing Christian's song "Christian Forever"

Playing Tyler's song, "Bubbles He Made"

When they were still toddlers, both Christian and Tyler had a fascination with trains. They loved Thomas Train, Lionel trains, National Geographic rail documentaries, and train books. We often took them to nearby tracks in anticipation of seeing a real one. A humorous family story took place when they were about two and three years old—both still in diapers. We have a long hallway between their bedrooms, and one day, they decided to make tracks from one end to the other—out of poop!

Another funny story is when our next-door neighbor called and asked, "Do you know where your boys are and what they're doing?"

"Well, not exactly," I answered.

She said, "They're throwing stuff out your bathroom window." Upon investigation, I found them tossing uncoiled rolls of toilet paper out the window. The air conditioner fan was directly below the window, and as they threw the rolls, the air pressure from the fan caused the paper to fly. I couldn't resist grabbing my camera to capture the Kodak moment. They spent the rest of the morning cleaning up the yard—and I was settling into fatherhood.

One of our treasured family traditions is Miracle Day. It started when Dianne and I celebrated our first Christmas together. Instead of placing mountains of presents under the tree, we decided that we would start a new tradition called Frivol Day (short for frivolous). We plan a day every year between Christmas and New Year's. We get up early, go out for a hearty breakfast, take a predetermined amount of money—cash in hand (an amount that we would have spent for Christmas split 50/50), and hang out all day shopping. Our choices can be practical or frivolous, and the rules were that the money has to be spent that day and no one is allowed to say, "Why in the world are you buying that?" Then we would top it off with a nice dinner.

Five years later, in 1999, our Frivol Day happened to be the same day we brought Christian home. We knew that Frivol Day would forever become Miracle Day! The following year, Tyler joined us. To this day, we have never missed spending a Miracle Day together, now splitting our funds four ways. It's the way we celebrate our family coming together.

To think the genesis of our happiness today was due to a flat tire in the rain. I could have driven right by, never knowing the joy of my children. Of all my experiences in life, this is by far the greatest. I found myself when I learned unconditional love.

Family photo

Woodism

Wisdom comes from seeing through the eyes of love
And listening with your heart

Two Masters

It was customary for astronaut crews to visit the various NASA field centers a few months post-flight to present their Silver Snoopy Awards (small pins based on the Peanut character "Snoopy") to team members who performed exemplary work on behalf of the mission and to debrief on the highlights of their mission.

NASA Public Affairs extended an open invitation to the "motivational" event to all NASA employees and contractors, stating, "We would appreciate having the support of all the NASA Marshall Team." Seating in the Morris Auditorium is limited to about 300 people. Dignitaries, resident space campers, and the local media were also invited. The debriefing normally lasted about one hour and was generally scheduled around the lunch hour. It consisted of a narrated video they shot on orbit—starting with the launch, highlights of the mission, and the descent—plus a Q&A session. After the event, the astronauts were on-hand for autographs and photo ops. It was always an honor to have the crew sign my handcrafted shuttle models.

STS-131 Crew members (right) Rick Mastracchio (Mission Specialist) and (left) Jim Dutton, Jr. (Pilot). Courtesy NASA

Our local management continued to discourage attendance at these and other NASA celebrations. We were paid to do our jobs, they said, not to attend functions. We were building a product that supported the mission and meeting the crew was a stark reminder of the importance of our work. And why not attend to show our appreciation for their dedication, hard work, and trust?

My position in Logistics allowed me to move about easily throughout NASA, and I organized my work schedule to attend these important events. I wanted to convey my support, but these functions also served as a release for me after the demanding, often daunting work on each flight, as well as a celebration of all of our efforts. I came away motivated and energized, ready for the next mission.

Most of all, I attended because I wanted firsthand documentation of the events and, on a grander scale, the Space Shuttle Program itself. I realized the historical significance of these debriefings: There would be only one STS-1 flight, only one STS-95 flight. It was a challenge assembling entire crews together, and I recognized each event as a once-in-a-lifetime opportunity. I took my Shuttle models and lithographs to have them autographed by the astronauts to create a historical record of the flights and the efforts put forth. The Shuttle Program represented the pinnacle of the aerospace community, and I wanted my models to reflect that excellence. I was bursting with enthusiasm to document for future generations how these brave men and women pushed the envelope of human understanding, the beginning of life in space.

Through my woodworking, I was able to make connections with the astronauts, and I got to know many crewmembers. The models were well received by the crews, and the astronauts seemed to enjoy signing them. On my second meeting with Scott Parazynski, for example, he said of my creations, "Scott, these are works of art." At another event, Eileen Collins smiled as she picked up a Sharpie to sign a model and said, "These are so beautiful. Are you sure you want me to sign this? I'm actually nervous to sign it." This woman, who had risked her life strapped to a controlled explosion, was apprehensive about signing the model with a Sharpie pen!

STS-93 Commander Eileen Collins signing
a shuttle model. Courtesy NASA

My office was filled with Shuttle memorabilia; it became a museum of sorts, featuring crew photos, autographed pictures, newspaper clippings, framed Shuttle stacks, Shuttle launches, unique shots from inside the tank, and the schematic drawing of the External Tank from Morley Robinson's wall. My collection entertained and educated visitors, including students, truck drivers, new employees, local politicians, and even astronauts. I also gathered handouts from NASA Public Affairs—press kits, NASA stickers, lithographs, flight stickers, patches, and posters. Everyone left my office with information, a positive message, a sticker for their window, or an orbiter cut-out for their child. Anyone who expressed an interest in the program, space history, or woodworking was told, "You need to go by Phillips' office." To my delight, I would often return to my office to find colleagues sharing my souvenirs with their guests.

Unfortunately, despite all of this, my managers saw me solely as working in logistics and discouraged me from pursuing anything outside of that narrow role—even though I consistently performed my job in an exemplary manner and my first priority was always to my work responsibilities. Yes, my passion fell outside my job scope, but I knew the program was finite, and I took on the mantle of collecting and documenting firsthand experiences to share with future generations.

Three months after Art Stevenson was appointed the new Marshall Space Flight Center director in 1998, he hosted his first crew event. The STS-95 crew came to MSFC for a post-flight celebration, and I was on hand with one of my models, in hopes of getting it signed by the crew. I arrived early to secure a front-row seat next to my NASA buddy, Ralph Young, who was also enthusiastic about these events. We were informed that the crew would not be signing autographs due to the large number of people at the event. The facility was filled to capacity, with nearly 1,000 people in attendance. Disappointed, I continued to maintain my front-row position in case a last-minute opportunity opened up.

To my astonishment, twenty minutes prior to the crew's arrival, a Public Affairs representative approached and asked if I would introduce the crew. I was surprised they asked me due to my contractor status, but I had built a positive reputation and could be counted on to welcome the crew with great enthusiasm. It was an opportunity I couldn't turn down. I carried my model to the front, and several people began asking me questions about it while we were waiting for the crew.

The moment arrived and in walked the Center Director Art Stevenson, Director of Protocol Sandra Turner, and the STS-95 crew, including Commander Curtis Brown, Pilot Steven Lindsey, Mission Specialists Stephen Robinson, Scott Parazynski, and Pedro Duque; and Payload Specialists Chiaki Mukai and John Glenn. Glenn, then seventy-seven, with this, his second space flight, became the oldest person to go into space. He had been one of the original Mercury astronauts—our first men to fly in space—and was also the first American to orbit the earth. At the time of STS-95, he was the sitting senator from Ohio.

Preparing to introduce the STS-95 crew (pictured r. to l.) Commander Curtis Brown, Mission Specialists Stephen Robinson, Scott Parazynski, and Pedro Duque; and Payload Specialist John Glenn. Courtesy NASA

I first met John Glenn and his wife, Annie, when they visited the Alabama Space and Rocket Center during his 1984 campaign for the US presidency. Unfortunately, his press secretary—my sister, Debbie—had already advanced to the next stop on the campaign trail and so didn't accompany them to Huntsville. As Glenn was greeting supporters, my parents and I introduced ourselves to Annie, and she arranged a few moments for us to speak with her husband before they were whisked away. I found them to be very warm and approachable.

At the ceremony for the STS-95 crew, I was hoping to speak with Sen. Glenn, but once again, he was hurried away to his next venue—a parade in downtown Huntsville in the crew's honor.

Marshall Star account of the STS-95 visit and parade
to honor the crew in downtown Huntsville

I wasn't able to get the model signed, but the experience was a thrill. Looking around the auditorium, I noticed one of my coworkers in attendance. I approached him and asked with a bit of sarcasm, "Does management know you're here?"

"Screw them!" he said. "John Glenn was my childhood hero."

I was now accepted by the NASA Public Affairs Office as a trusted participant, rather than merely a spectator. When I learned that the STS-93 crew would be visiting MSFC in October 1999, I contacted Public Affairs to see if I could participate. This had been an important mission at MSFC because this is where the Chandra Telescope Program had been managed. The Chandra X-ray Observatory, the most sophisticated instrument built to-date, was designed to observe X-rays from high-energy regions of the universe, such as hot gas in the remnants of exploded stars. It sought to answer such serious astrophysical questions as what the universe is made of. I suggested to NASA that we do something special and volunteered to create a shuttle model for the crew to autograph and donate to the Marshall Team. I was thrilled when Art Stevenson sanctioned the idea and suggested that it be put on display for the upcoming NASA administrators' visit.

This opportunity kicked off many firsts for me: It was my first behind-the-scenes photo op (along with Dianne) with an astronaut crew. It was also the first of many meetings with Eileen Collins, the first female Shuttle commander. She asked me about my models, including about where I get the woods and what inspired me. I told her, "Just as you see no borders in orbit as you observe the Earth, I gather woods from each country and blend them together as a unique representation of your mission." When I asked Dianne how it felt meeting the crew, she smiled and said, "I felt proud to be an American."

STS-93 crew (l. to r.) Mission Specialist Cady Coleman, (Dianne), Pilot Jeffrey Ashby, (Scott), Commander Eileen Collins, and Mission Specialist Michael Tognini. Courtesy NASA

The model, along with a photo of the crew signing it, was put on display in NASA Marshall Space Flight Center Headquarters. A picture of NASA Administrator Dan Golden was later taken next to my artwork and published in the *Marshall Star*.

MSFC Center Director Art Stevenson and NASA Administrator Dan Golden. Courtesy NASA

This was the first time I was in the *Marshall Star*, an official weekly publication started in 1960, during the Wernher von Braun days, to recognize and document the NASA missions supported at MSFC, including the moon landings, Skylab, the Space Shuttle Program, the International Space Station, the Hubble Telescope, and Chandra, to name a few. I was honored to be recognized by the MSFC Team, particularly as a contractor. Several years later, I had an opportunity to meet astronauts Carl Waltz and Dan Bursch, who served on the fourth expedition to the International Space Station. I introduced myself and Waltz said, "Scott, we already know you. We read about your work in the *Marshall Star* in orbit!"

After my photo appeared in the *Marshall Star*, my management reminded me of their previous pronouncement. Since they had little interest in my artwork, I did not tell them that I would be meeting, on my own time, the STS-93 crew to have them autograph one of my models. I didn't anticipate that the meeting would be featured in the *Marshall Star*. I found myself in the proverbial hot seat with a stern reminder: "You're paid to do Logistics and that's it."

A year later, in November 2000, I was displaying my models at a woodworking event in downtown Huntsville. It was Veterans' Day, and Art Stevenson was on the NASA float as the grand marshal. He had been informed about the woodworking event and stopped by my booth. He told me, "When I saw you at the STS-95 debriefing, I decided I wanted to own one of your models. Do you have any available?" I showed him the last one I had made for the year and explained the documentation that came with the model. He said, "This is outstanding! This is great work. I'm proud that you're able to do this. Your work is very inspirational to the overall Shuttle Program." I was excited to share my passion with him and believed he was trying to change the longstanding NASA culture of not associating with non-NASA personnel. I was disappointed, however, that he left before meeting my family.

Dianne showed up thirty minutes later, pushing a double stroller with Christian up front and newborn Tyler asleep in the caboose.

A few weeks later, Stevenson invited me to a private meeting in his office where he planned to have the STS-92 crew, which was the hundredth Shuttle flight, sign the model he had purchased. He formally introduced me to each crew member, saying, "I want to introduce you to Scott Phillips, the creator of this model and an External Tank team member. He's here to assist in getting it autographed by you, but first, he's going to share with you about his passion and his work on the Shuttle Program." I described the flight element that we manufactured at MSFC and gave a little history about the composite nose cone. Commander Brian Duffy is very witty and commented on my enthusiasm, "Wow! You're really into this!"

I answered, "Yes, I am!" and we all had a good laugh. I then guided the crew in signing the model. My bias is always for the commander to sign on the External Tank, which he did. The crew appeared to be impressed with my presentation and the director was beaming with pride.

Scott and MSFC Director Art Stevenson with STS-92 crew (l. to r.) Pilot Pam Melroy, Mission Specialists Leroy Chiao and Jeff Wisoff, and Commander Brian Duffy. Courtesy NASA

Then Stevenson invited me to join them for lunch. All I could think about was the last time I got slammed for spending time with an astronaut crew. I was reluctant to accept, knowing the Federal Code of Regulations about preferential treatment from a customer. But on the other hand, how could I decline such an invitation? And it *was* my lunch hour. I replied, "I would be honored." As I glanced around the director's private dining room at the STS-92 crew and top NASA leadership team, I shuddered to realize I was the only contractor present.

During introductions around the table, I was hesitant to divulge my company affiliation. Luckily, when it came to my turn, the crew laughed and said, "We already know you, Scott!" That eased my tension. It further relaxed me that I was sitting next to Dr. Jan Davis, a former astronaut who lives in Huntsville and whom I had known for several years. The other attendees included crew members Brian Duffy, Pam Melroy, Jeff Wisoff, Leroy Chiao, and Stevenson's management team. Conversation was pleasantly informal and directed toward the crew's impressions of the vehicle performance. Brian Duffy said, "We were hauling ass with your propulsion system, and we want to thank you for that." Stevenson chimed in with, "It's enough to run 17,000 pickup trucks in Alabama." Leroy Chiao laughed so hard that he accidentally dropped his elbow on the fork handle sitting on his plate and flipped a pea into the air. We all enjoyed another good laugh.

A final guest entered the room, our main customer, Shuttle Projects Director Alex McCool. McCool and I had worked together many times during the External Tank testing phase and more recently as a result of my Logistics functions. Because it was unusual to see a contractor in a private meeting with the NASA executive management team, I wasn't surprised when he recognized me and asked, "What are you doing here?" I told him that Art Stevenson had invited me to get his Shuttle model autographed. I knew McCool had a direct pipeline to my director and could easily report me. If he did, I would pay hugely, perhaps with my job. After lunch, I was relieved to spot a wicker basket on a side table with a note taped to the side that said "lunch donations." I happily contributed to avoid a potential impropriety, but I spent the week looking over my shoulder.

Because of my good standing with the center director, an interesting opportunity was presented to me. The Photo Lab asked me to model NASA logo sweaters and T-shirts available for purchase in the MSFC Exchange catalog. I was convinced that my company would be promoted in a positive light, and the photos would be shot during my personal time. I was intrigued and decided to do it.

I was told there would be a dozen or so shots taken, but because there would be other models, only one or two shots of me were likely to make it into the catalog; however, Web sites were just beginning to show up on the horizon, and I was unaware that the catalog would be posted online with my picture splashed throughout. When I saw this, I became concerned about my decision and the potential ramifications.

Several months after my modeling gig, to my delight, I attended a huge NASA celebration picnic that had *actually* been sanctioned by my management. It was the twentieth anniversary of the STS-1 flight with crew members Bob Crippen and John Young. I had approached Art Stevenson about having the crew sign two models, one of which I would donate to NASA to commemorate the anniversary. Because of the thousands of people in attendance, it was announced that there would be no autographs granted that day, and even though I had staged the models earlier that morning in Stevenson's office, I wasn't sure if the plan would actually materialize.

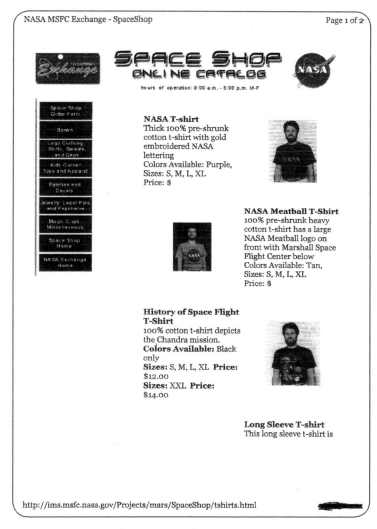

SPACE SHOP
ONLINE CATALOG
hours of operation: 9:00 a.m. - 5:00 p.m. M-F

Space Shop Order Form

Books

Logo Clothing, Shirts, Sweats, and Caps

Kids Corner, Toys and Apparel

Patches and Decals

Jewelry, Lapel Pins, and Keychains

Mugs, Cups, Miscellaneous

Space Shop Home

NASA Exchange Home

NASA T-shirt
Thick 100% pre-shrunk cotton t-shirt with gold embroidered NASA lettering
Colors Available: Purple,
Sizes: S, M, L, XL
Price: $

NASA Meatball T-Shirt
100% pre-shrunk heavy cotton t-shirt has a large NASA Meatball logo on front with Marshall Space Flight Center below
Colors Available: Tan,
Sizes: S, M, L, XL
Price: $

History of Space Flight T-Shirt
100% cotton t-shirt depicts the Chandra mission.
Colors Available: Black only
Sizes: S, M, L, XL **Price:** $12.00
Sizes: XXL **Price:** $14.00

Long Sleeve T-shirt
This long sleeve t-shirt is

http://ims.msfc.nasa.gov/Projects/mars/SpaceShop/tshirts.html

MSFC Online Apparel Catalog

At the picnic, everyone who had worked on STS-1 was asked to stand. A NASA colleague glanced over at me with a surprised look on his face and asked, "Phillips, how old *are* you?"

I responded, "Old enough to have worked on STS-1!"

Just as I was recounting the story of being the last guy out of the first External Tank, my cell phone rang. It was NASA Public Affairs Office, requesting me to meet the director in his office after the picnic for autographs and an exclusive photo op with Bob Crippen and John Young. Of the thousands of people at the function, I had been singled out to have a personal audience with these two historical icons as they autographed the models.

As I was waiting outside the office, my mind drifted back to STS-1 when I was exiting the External Tank for the last time and had pulled the "remove before flight" ribbon. Here I was, twenty years later, getting ready to come full circle. The doors opened and the NASA photographer and I were invited in. I was introduced as a team member from Lockheed Martin and the craftsman who had built the models. John Young shook my hand and said, "I was a model builder as a young boy. I really appreciate your work." I then shook Bob Crippen's hand, and he, too, complimented me on my craftsmanship. "Your work is outstanding and inspirational," he said. The NASA photographer took pictures of our introduction and continued to document them autographing the models and receiving gifts of appreciation from Art Stevenson. The photographer looked over at me and said, "Scott, you're next in the shot." As I walked toward them, John Young chimed in, "Let's do it with the shuttle models." They set down their mementos and picked up the models for the photo op.

I was nearly overcome with emotion as I stood next to them. After all, they were my heroes. It felt surreal. My knees were trembling as I stood next to the commander of STS-1 and the ninth man to walk on the moon. For a guy who once dreamed of being part of something really important, something that made a difference, this turned out to be one of my finest moments.

(l. to r.) Art Stevenson, Bob Crippen, John Young, and Scott. Courtesy NASA

I donated one of the autographed models to the Marshall director's office, and he proudly displayed it on the conference table in his office for as long as he was in that position. It periodically showed up on local television and in the *Huntsville Times* and *Marshall Star* during notable interviews around the table. This was unquestionably a win-win situation, and I was honored to support him with an art piece that he admired.

The photo taken of me with Bob Crippen, John Young, and Art Stevenson did come back to sting me. A couple days after the picnic, my company director called me. He said, "I need to see you. Come to my office." On my way into the meeting, I was informed by his executive assistant that he had a copy of the picture taken in Stevenson's office. Knowing that the celebration picnic had been sanctioned by my company, I assumed I was about to get kudos for my meeting with the center director and the STS-1 crew. I entered his office smiling. I noticed he was leaning back in his chair behind his expansive desk with a scowl on his face. He began by saying, "Our participation in the NASA function was sanctioned through the lunch hour." He leaned forward and showed me the photo. "Do you see anything that stands out about this picture?" he asked. I looked at the picture and said, "No." He responded, "Look at the clock. It's five minutes past our lunch hour." I caught the picture in midair as he flung it toward me across his desk. I was stunned. He barked, "Put those five minutes on your time card. That's all." The air was immediately sucked out of my tires. I had fallen into his trap. I realized that it was now personal. I feigned a polite level of contrition, but I was resolute to continue my vision. I knew the historic value of experiencing and documenting this program. I began investing my personal vacation leave during crew events. And the NASA photographers always made sure there were no clocks in my background.

Meeting with the STS-1 crew propelled my passion for collecting and preserving history to a new height. I felt empowered, yet I had a growing concern about a potential conflict of interest since my artwork was now a known commodity. I contacted the Lockheed Martin legal department to assure this was not the case. They determined that no conflict of interest existed provided it did not interfere with my work. Even with that disclosure on file, I determined that all future extracurricular contact with the Center director and crews would now have to be totally off the radar.

I felt like I was living a double life. I was answering to two masters. I found myself meeting with high-level NASA personnel periodically to discuss details when my Shuttle models were commissioned for upcoming retirements. And whenever one of my models was presented, I was normally invited to the function. I made sure I attended these functions on my personal time.

I began to learn all I could about NASA protocol and the delicate and timely choreography of controlled events. I knew that would be my ticket to future gatherings. I was a willing student, mentored by the seasoned protocol staff, and became a trusted participant in NASA events. The Public Affairs office recognized and appreciated my artwork, and they helped by giving me heads-up to upcoming functions and making sure I received official photos to document the occasions. Their confidence in me grew with each successful protocol, and I felt confident my vision for documenting and preserving the Shuttle's legacy was secure.

I was requested to attend an off-site NASA ceremony in December 2001 at which Art Stevenson was presenting one of my models to his boss, Joe Rothenberg, the Associate Administrator of Space Flight, who was retiring. Since the event was being held off-site after hours at the Space and Rocket Center museum, I was comfortable knowing that I was, for once, beyond the clutches of my autocratic company management. All eyes were on my Shuttle model as it was presented to Mr. Rothenberg.

After the ceremony, as everyone began spilling into the reception area, a NASA Public Affairs representative approached me and asked if I would remain present for a photo with Mr. Rothenberg. He wanted to personally thank me and get a photo of us with his model. As I was walking through the crowded museum, I was stunned when I spotted my company director walking toward me with a cocktail in his hand since he typically did not attend NASA functions. As he approached me, he sarcastically said, "I suppose you'll be making a model for the President of the United States someday." The moment I finished voicing the words, "I'm working on it," the NASA representative interrupted to tell me that Mr. Rothenberg was ready for the photo. I politely excused myself and headed toward the reception line. As I was posing with Mr. Rothenberg with the camera lights flashing, I glanced out toward the crowd and could see a look of disbelief as well as agitation on my director's face. Whether it was professional jealousy, control, or simply a personal bone, I knew I would be paid back in spades when I returned to my office.

Scott with NASA Associate Administrator for Space
Flight, Joe Rothenberg. Courtesy NASA

A year earlier, in 2000, I had submitted a patent application for
a device called a Magnetic Back-to-Back Strain Gauge Locator.
A tornado was approaching MSFC one day and I was waiting
out the storm in the basement of one of our block houses—thick
concrete steel bunkers with steel doors and bullet-proof glass
normally used for protection while testing rocket engines. While
waiting out the storm, I was contemplating a problem we were
experiencing when trying to find the center of the x-y axis from
the outside to the inside of the External Tank for a true back-to-
back location while laying strain gauges. On a nearby drafting
table, I sketched a crude diagram of an idea I had that could
possibly solve our problem. Within six months, I had completed
an abstract, built a prototype, and submitted it to my company.

The idea was determined to be a patentable product. Lockheed
Martin pursued the laborious patent process, and two years later,
I was awarded my patent. As it turned out, it was one of only
twenty-five full patents awarded off the External Tank program.
Naturally, all intellectual property originating while working

under contract is owned by NASA, and my reward was a cash bonus from Lockheed Martin. A check was cut around the time of the photo op with Joe Rothenberg, but my director kept it in his drawer for several months. When he finally decided to give it to me, there was no fanfare, no formal recognition. That, no doubt, was my payback.

Patent #6,137,281

The online catalog Web site finally showed up on my director's computer screen one day when he was shopping for NASA apparel. I wish I could have been a fly on the wall when he saw me wearing the very T-shirt he planned to purchase. The time bomb had exploded. He demanded to know when, why, where, and how that photo came about. I explained that it happened several years earlier under a previous manager and that he had sanctioned it. Not the entire truth, but I wasn't in the mood for a confrontation with him about his damn T-shirt.

Woodism

One man can make a million people miserable
but a million people can't make one man happy

Shot for the Moon, Hit the Foot

My mentor, Henry Hankal, once told me, "Anyone can do twenty years on a job, but beyond that, you better have a passion, because that's what will carry you through the tough times to the end." I didn't understand what he meant when he said it, but in December 2002, as I was entering my twenty-fifth year with the Space Shuttle Program, it made perfect sense. The negative attitude from my management toward my vision to document firsthand experiences became increasingly more caustic. Fortunately, my desire for collecting and model building was at an all-time high, and I was able to neutralize the adverse effects of my obtuse environment. I had the ear of the director of the Marshall Space Flight Center, and my ideas were flowing.

My final "sanctioned" event with Art Stevenson was in October 2002 when NASA headquarters decided to relocate MSFC Deputy Director Jim Kennedy to Kennedy Space Center. A shuttle model was commissioned for him and autographed by the MSFC management team. I had hit a homerun.

Jim Kennedy receiving a shuttle model. Courtesy NASA

The following month, I received advanced word that the Apollo 17 crew would be making an appearance at MSFC to celebrate the thirtieth anniversary of their moon landing. The visit was symbolically scheduled for December 11, the exact date of the final moon landing. I was excited at the possibility of seeing Gene Cernan and Harrison Schmitt, two of my boyhood heroes. Cernan was the commander on Apollo 17 and the eleventh man to walk on the moon. Schmitt, who served as senator from New Mexico from 1977-83, was the twelfth man on the moon as well as the first and only scientist. Interestingly, Schmitt returned to the lunar lander first, which made Cernan the last man on the moon.

With a unique idea and a short lead time, I approached Art Stevenson with the concept of creating two shuttle-shaped lunar surface models to celebrate their visit. My idea would then take it to another level and use external tank exterior insulation foam to create the moon surface. I planned to use indigenous stones from the Marshall Rocket Park on Redstone Arsenal, sprayed silver to simulate moon rocks, and a miniature moon rover, which was the lunar-surface vehicle managed by MSFC during the moon program. My vision was to show that without the Apollo

Program—there would be no Shuttle! The one-of-a-kind art pieces with the theme "building off the shoulders of giants" would be autographed by the Apollo crew. One would be donated to the upcoming Tenth Annual Great Moonbuggy Race in Huntsville and awarded to the winning team; the second art piece would remain in my private collection.

The Great Moonbuggy Race is an annual event supported by MSFC at the Space and Rocket Center. Teams of high school and college students build non-motorized, two-person vehicles to specification for a moon excursion. The top team receives cash prizes, publicity, and a team award. Stevenson's assistant contacted me a few days later, saying, "Art turned down the idea. He feels your project is too commercial." I had expected a positive response from him, and when that didn't happen, I was surprised and disappointed. I felt that because the idea was presented through someone else, his decision was due to his lack of understanding about the idea of supporting the tenth anniversary of the Moonbuggy Race and continued to move forward with my vision. Utilizing my good standing with Public Affairs, I presented my idea to them. I thought if it became their idea, it could force a compromise on his part. I could clearly see the win-win situation, and they did too.

Public Affairs took ownership of the idea and orchestrated a plan that I would be on standby with the lunar models in the Heritage Gallery adjacent to the auditorium where the Apollo 17 crew would be speaking. They scheduled a ten-minute window for me to secure the signatures and have pictures taken before they entered the auditorium. I assumed the plan would "fly or die" when they coordinated the protocol schedule with Stevenson. I was highly motivated by the thought that the last two men who walked on the moon in the twentieth century, Gene Cernan and Harrison Schmitt, would be signing my art pieces.

On the morning prior to the Apollo 17 crew visit, I was on pins and needles. I had a sense that Stevenson might not have been included in the Public Affairs plan, and I was apprehensive about moving forward, knowing I could be in direct defiance of his decision. I was quite surprised when I received a last-minute phone call requesting my presence in the Heritage Gallery to meet with the Apollo 17 crew with the models. Knowing I had a only ten minutes and aware of the fact that Art Stevenson would be on stage warming up the Marshall team in the adjacent auditorium during that time, I convinced myself the plan would go without a hitch. I allowed my passion for documenting history to overrule my sensibility and accepted the invitation.

An hour later, I was with a NASA photographer waiting in the Gallery with the lunar models when I saw astronauts Cernan and Schmitt being escorted through the main door and greeted by high-ranking dignitaries in a receiving line. As they entered the Gallery, I was introduced as a Space Shuttle team member and a local artist. I proceeded to explain how the models were made and shared the theme, "building off the shoulders of giants." They loved the idea! I explained that one autographed model would be donated to the Great Moonbuggy Race and the other would remain in my personal collection, not to be sold.

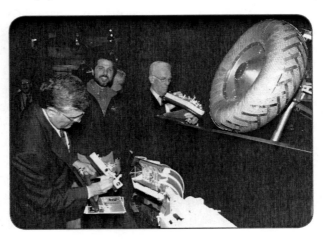

Harrison Schmitt and Gene Cernan autographing one-of-a-kind Moonbuggy art pieces. Courtesy NASA

After they autographed the models and the NASA photographer finished taking pictures, I packed up and was ready to make my exit. Just then the MSFC coordinator for the Moonbuggy Race arrived in the Gallery and requested a picture with the astronauts, myself, and the lunar model. I thought, *Crap! There's no time for this!* As she was removing the model from the box, Art Stevenson entered the Gallery. The glare on his face confirmed he had definitely not sanctioned the Public Affairs plan. My stomach bottomed out. I had anticipated a quiet meeting with the astronauts and carefully calculated the time. But I didn't anticipate the number of people that would be in the room, all the cameras flashing, or a last-minute photo request. Time had run out and the situation had gotten out of control. Without saying a word and undetected by anyone else, Stevenson's piercing stare forced me out of my position. He stepped in the picture with the coordinator and the two astronauts. Standing off to the side, I felt a wave of nausea as I thought of what this could mean—not only the end of his support but possibly worse.

Just then, the protocol director reentered the room. Stevenson promptly went over and discretely reprimanded her. As he and the entourage headed to the auditorium for the presentation, he turned back, looked me in the eye, and pointed his finger. "I'll deal with you later," he said. To say I was concerned is a huge understatement. A contractor cannot tick off the center director and get away unscathed. That was on Friday, and I spent the entire weekend expecting the worst. I kept the details of the meeting—and my fears—to myself. I placed the autographed lunar models on a shelf in my workshop and took out my frustration on the task of replacing our pesky dishwasher—cursing every small obstacle.

Moonbuggy art piece autographed by Gene Cernan
and Harrison Schmitt. Courtesy NASA

The following week, I went through the motions at work and cringed at every meeting, waiting for the other shoe to drop. I finally received an e-mail from Stevenson expressing his displeasure. His last words in the e-mail were, "You let your passion overrule your judgment." He was right. I had what I felt was a great idea and my intentions were good, but when I thought he had turned me down because he didn't understand the vision, I reached too far. I let my enthusiasm overrule my good sense, and I lost much of the goodwill I had built up with him. That failure cut me to my core.

I kept a low profile and suffered in silence. One week followed another and then another. I began feeling paranoid, fearing my IT guys would discover Stevenson's e-mail and decide to elevate the issue to my management. I felt so badly that I didn't even mention the incident to Dianne. Art Stevenson and I had developed a relationship of respect and admiration, and I was disappointed in myself. I dug deep, examining my actions in light of his past support and generosity. I never spoke with him again, and I am thankful he chose to offer me grace. Even though my vision failed and the second lunar model never made it to the Moonbuggy Race, I am forever reminded by these two art pieces of an important lesson that I learned: You may have a great idea, but if you don't articulate it well and get everyone on board, it will not succeed.

Woodism

When you shoot for the moon, make sure your passion doesn't overrule your sensibility!

Columbia and the
Beginning of the End

On the morning of February 1, 2003, the Space Shuttle Columbia was returning from a sixteen-day marathon mission during which they had performed more than eighty earth and space science experiments. During its approach to Kennedy Space Center, I heard that Columbia was "coming late" in flying over where they had been expected. The words shook me. Next came an announcement from Houston Mission Control that there was excessive heating in the interior of the wing structure.

I well knew the inherent risks for both the ascent and descent of the Shuttle, but we always considered the launch more hazardous because it involved the dynamics of the propulsion elements. The landing was viewed as more of a completion of the mission, a celebration of sorts. Reality struck when, flashing across my television screen, I saw amateur photographs of debris trails in the skies over Texas. I was paralyzed with disbelief.

Lost in the disaster were Commander Rick Husband; Pilot William McCool; Mission Specialists Dr. David Brown, Dr. Laurel Clark, Kalpana Chawla, and Michael Anderson; and Payload Specialist Ilan Ramon, the first Israeli astronaut.

STS-107 Crewmembers. Courtesy NASA

Unlike the tragedy of the Challenger, I watched this accident unfold in real time, at home on the NASA Channel. Although it was customary for me to see a mission through to the landing, Columbia, in particular, had always held a special place for me. It was the heaviest orbiter in the fleet and also the heaviest influence on my career. I thought of it as "my orbiter." It had flown with the first External Tank shortly after I exited the tank and pulled the "Remove Before Flight" ribbon. It flew on my Launch Honoree mission STS-62. When it made a special visit to Huntsville in 1994, I helped lead a tour for the general public at the Huntsville International Airport. I also had the pleasure of meeting the last successful commander of Columbia, Scott Altman, STS-109, after the Hubble repair mission.

Scott with Orbiter Columbia

Within minutes of the first reports, I began receiving automated phone calls from our company president notifying us of the status. When my phone rang again, I assumed it was yet another call from our phone system with further information about the orbiter. I was surprised to hear our HR representative on the other end. She was calling to inform me that my office mate of twelve years, Carol Duncan, was found dead at her home as a result of heart failure. I buckled under the weight of this double whammy.

I recalled that the last thing I had said to Carol was a reminder to watch the landing, and I immediately thought that the news of Columbia might have caused her attack. Later, however, I learned that she had died hours prior to the accident. At least she had been spared the knowledge of that tragedy.

The Space Shuttle Program, as we knew it, came to a screeching halt that day. My work continued, but we were unable to hire a replacement for Carol and her work fell to me. Add to that, my other coworker had retired about six months prior, and Carol and I were already picking up the slack in our office from that loss. I was carrying the workload of a three-person operation all alone, even as I struggled with the emotional burden.

President George W. Bush appointed the Columbia Accident Investigation Board (CAIB), headed by retired four-star Admiral Harold W. Gehman Jr., who was formerly the NATO Supreme Allied Commander of the Atlantic as well as cochairman of the Department of Defense review of the attack on the USS *Cole*. After six months, the CAIB report identified the physical cause of the loss of Columbia and its crew as a breach in the Thermal Protection System (TPS) on the leading edge of the left wing. Eighty-two seconds after launch, a piece of insulation foam, the size of a large suitcase, had separated from the left bipod ramp of the External Tank and hit the wing at more than 1,600 miles per hour. During reentry, this breach in the TPS allowed superheated air to seep in the hole, weakening the aluminum structure on the wing until increasing aerodynamic forces caused loss of control, failure of the wing, and breakup of the Orbiter.

Columbia Accident Investigation Board Report

The piece of insulation foam that broke off the left bipod ramp

When we lost Columbia, along with our seven courageous astronauts, it started a process that would eventually end the program. Unlike with the Challenger, this time it was our product that had been the cause. The bottom line, which we all knew deep down was imminent, the CAIB report recommended a full recertification of all elements of the Shuttle by 2010. This would mean going back and examining and re-certifying all vendors, materials, procedures, and processes over the previous several decades. The time required and the enormous cost involved would be prohibitive and unsustainable for the production lines. The program would be brought to a standstill during the recertification process, thereby losing valuable skill sets and forcing small vendors to close.

Because the Shuttle was relied on to do the heavy lifting for the construction elements of the International Space Station, NASA and the president decided to complete the remaining twenty flights to satisfy our partnership requirements. The road back for the "Return to Flight" mission, the first flight post-Columbia, was a long and arduous process. Our goal on the External Tank program was to reduce insulation foam and potential ice buildup in critical areas on the orbiter side of the tank. We began a round-the-clock operation to affect these changes.

After dissecting another tank in production, the Foreign Object Displacement Program found an accumulation of objects—popsicle sticks, badges, rags, and coins—that had accidentally become embedded in the foam, thereby diminishing the integrity of the foam application. New quality procedures and mandatory training were put in place to reduce the amount of debris in the final tank assembly.

Building the External Tank was a complicated process. Supervisors and technicians dealt constantly with issues associated with multiple tanks, often moving between tanks as their skills were needed. When it became apparent that one person should oversee all activity on each tank, a new position was created as an added layer of support between the floor supervisor and the technicians and engineers. Tank Specific Project Managers, affectionately known as "Missile Moms," came from various departments to facilitate efficient problem-solving, making sure all the paperwork was in order and handling all the nitpicky details. They were neutral in that their focus was purely on quality and safety, and they were highly motivated, knowing their names were on the final signoff to the customer.

We were struggling, individually and as a team, but we continued to move forward, hoping the program would one day resume its full capability. The belief that the Shuttle Program would again be strong kept us going.

I was involved in a comprehensive plan to modify and improve the tank's foam architecture. For more than two years, I had sole responsibility for logistical support requirements, a weight that was heavy both mentally and physically. MSFC was responsible for the research and development of the new foam process and redesign of the External Tank. I was responsible for procurement, shipping, receiving, and ensuring quality of equipment and materials. Adding to the load, a few months later, a coworker and friend, Nathan McCormick, was killed in a tragic automobile accident. In an already emotionally charged year, this challenged me ever further.

Even as I was adjusting to this new normal, I received a blow more brutal than I could have imagined.

In July 2004, my father passed away unexpectedly during surgery to repair an aortic aneurysm. My heart ached. It was my breaking point. The emotional traumas finally overwhelmed me and began taking a toll on my health. On several occasions, I briefly lost consciousness when the scales were tipped. Dianne and I got to know the local emergency room drill intimately.

Because of these episodes, I was in danger of losing my professional certifications for handling sensitive and heavy equipment. I knew that others in the industry had faced similar jeopardy. Over the years, I had read most of the autobiographies written by astronauts; many recount medical issues that were kept hidden out of fear of losing their flight status.

I forged ahead, maintaining a low profile. After one incident, my manager decided to accompany us to the emergency room. Dianne knew he was waiting for a diagnosis, and she assured him there would not be one. He just stood there with a puzzled look on his face. Eventually, it was determined that my episodes were due solely to stress. The weeks turned into months.

I finally succumbed to the overwhelming call back into my creative cave, my workshop. Armed with my undaunted passion, I sought to create something unique to channel both my personal and professional grief and sustain me through my healing process, something on a grand scale.

One day, I received a call from NASA inquiring about the logistics of safely shipping a time capsule that the City of Huntsville had recently exhumed. The capsule had been buried beneath the courthouse lawn during Huntsville's 150th birthday celebration in 1955 with instructions to open it for the city's bicentennial celebration. Among the contents, local politicians, high school students, and the commanding general at Redstone Arsenal had contributed predictions about what Huntsville would be like in 2005. Their predictions included one that we would land a man on Mars by 1985, and Mayor R. B. "Speck" Searcy predicted that Redstone Arsenal would become a mecca for scientists from around the world. With the formulation of MSFC in 1960, that prediction did come true.

When the capsule was unearthed, they discovered a waterlogged vault, although some of the contents had been sealed in pouches blocking out moisture. Officials needed to know how to stabilize and ship these sensitive—and wet—materials. My suggestion was to flash freeze the contents in dry ice and place them in a wax container for shipping and then to use an autoclave oven at the destination to dry and stabilize the materials. My suggestions were employed, and the materials were forensically restored through a drying process by a company in New York that had previously restored artifacts from the *Titanic*.

This important historical event inspired me to create a Space Shuttle time capsule. I envisioned a twelve-inch hollow rosewood cube serving as a base to one of my shuttle models, perched vertically in a launch position, to honor the Return to Flight STS-114 mission as well as the memory of the Columbia crew, my father, and my two deceased coworkers. I approached NASA Public Affairs Office and the new Center Director, Dave King. Everyone was on board and my idea took flight like a rising phoenix. It took exactly one year to design, build, and execute my plan.

During this time, we were all working at a punishing pace, including evenings, weekends, and holidays to achieve Return to Flight on schedule. Our hard work paid off when, on July 26, 2005, the STS-114 crew roared back into space on Discovery and returned safely eleven days later.

STS-114 Discovery "Return to Flight"
rolling to Pad 39A. Courtesy NASA

STS-114 Discovery "Return to Flight"
Artifact. Courtesy Robert Pearlman

The following November, the STS-114 crew visited MSFC post-flight from their historic mission. The Marshall team and STS-114 crew were invited to gather pictures, flight patches, commemorative coins, and personal notes and memorabilia honoring this specific mission as well as the future of space exploration to place inside the time capsule. I was in charge of packing and sealing the capsule, where the contents would remain until it is opened again on a predicted historical event of world significance: the landing of an American astronaut on Mars. We included many predictions of when that might happen. STS-114 astronaut Soichi Noguchi included a picture of his family and said to me, "I hope I am here to participate in its opening when we land a man on Mars!" The unique difference with this capsule is that it is displayed above ground as an art piece and a visual reminder to the next generations.

Space Shuttle STS-114 Time Capsule. Courtesy NASA

A piece of information about the Huntsville time capsule had caught my attention: The individual heading the Bicentennial Commission, while still a young girl in 1955, had been told by her father that he had slipped something into the time capsule for her. She waited fifty years, and to her great disappointment, she discovered that no such item was in the exhumed capsule. This gave me an inspiration, and the last things I made sure were placed in the capsule prior to sealing it were love letters to my two boys, Christian and Tyler. My healing, as I had hoped, came gradually through the process of building the time capsule model.

NASA Public Affairs asked me to plan the time capsule ceremony to follow the official crew debriefing to the Marshall Team at MSFC Headquarters. I strove to create a celebration that was both commemorative and symbolic. Crewmembers, Eileen Collins, James Kelly, Soichi Noguchi, and Wendy Lawrence reverently autographed the time capsule with a pen inscribed with his or her name, which was then presented to four fifth-grade honor students who showed a special interest in science, a symbolic passing the torch to the next generation—potential candidates for the Mars landing!

Space Shuttle Time Capsule Ceremony:
Passing the torch to the next generation. Courtesy NASA

(l. to r.) Pilot James Kelly, Commander Eileen Collins,
Scott, Dianne, Mission Specialists Soichi Noguchi
and Wendy Lawrence. Courtesy NASA

Dianne and I attended the ceremony as special guests. I was thrilled to sit next to someone who had inspired me in my own journey, Homer Hickam, author of the best-selling memoir *Rocket Boys*, which was the inspiration for the movie *October Sky*. He gave me a copy of his book with the inscription "To Shuttleman from Rocket Boy."

I am proud to say that the time capsule is on permanent display in the Heritage Gallery at MSFC NASA Headquarters, securing the Shuttle's legacy, until that historic day when we land an American astronaut on Mars.

During the twenty-nine months that the program was shut down, many new tools and upgrades were developed. The process was extremely complex but brilliantly executed. There would now be a "launch on need" shuttle, meaning one that could be ready within a couple of weeks as a backup rescue in case of irreparable damage during launch or in flight. Upon reaching orbit, on the first day of a mission, the astronauts would deploy from the cargo bay a scanning boom that would view the orbiter from top to bottom to detect any damage during ascent. An on-orbit repair technique was developed that would require an astronaut to perform an extravehicular activity to apply a caulking-like material to repair any minor damage. As an added safety precaution, the return flight path to KSC was slightly altered to reduce flying over heavily populated areas. And there would be the safe harbor of the International Space Station for all remaining flights—except those to the Hubble Telescope due to its different orbital inclination and inaccessible location from the Space Station.

Because of the Hubble mission's unique position, the then-current NASA Administrator, Sean O'Keefe, in spite of the upgrades, decided to cancel the final Hubble repair mission in 2004, which was a huge blow to the scientific community around the world. That decision would render the telescope to space junk that would eventually fall back to earth, and we would lose our eye into the universe. But O'Keefe considered the mission too risky, and that opinion was also supported by chief engineer and former Hubble astronaut John Grumsfeld. O'Keefe resigned his position in December 2004, prior to the scheduled STS-114 Return to Flight mission, but stayed on board until a successor was named.

O'Keefe had come from the Office of Management and Budget and was known as the "bean counter" hired by NASA to get their financial house in order. Unfortunately, early in his appointment, the Columbia accident occurred, thereby thrusting him in a position outside of his expertise. However, he understood the importance of expanding our space program, and to his credit, he convinced President Bush to set NASA on a new course, "A Vision of Space Exploration." This vision sought to implement a sustained and affordable program of human and robotic space exploration, and to return to the moon by the year 2020 in preparation for human exploration of Mars and beyond. President Bush, in his first term, ordered NASA to determine how we could significantly increase our abilities to operate outside of earth's environment and to develop technologies needed to open up the space frontier while conducting fundamental sciences. He stated, "This is a journey not a race." Under O'Keefe, the vision of the Constellation program was created and would include manned missions to the International Space Station, the moon, and Mars. He made the decision to cancel the Space Shuttle by 2010 circumventing the possibility of recertification recommended by the CAIB Report. I was deeply saddened to hear that my beloved Shuttle Program would end. Yet I was cautiously encouraged by the expanded goal of going back to the moon and on to Mars.

Poised for advancing the new vision, NASA was ready for a true rocket scientist and visionary to take the helm. We were elated when Dr. Mike Griffin was sworn in as the eleventh NASA administrator in April 2005. Mike not only had seven degrees to his credit, but also he had recently served as head of the Space Department at Johns Hopkins University and earlier had been chief engineer at NASA and deputy for technology at the Strategic Defense Initiative organization.

Griffin had been NASA administrator for only three months when STS-114 roared into space. Unfortunately, the mission was marred due to losing a small piece of foam off the tank. It happened late in the flight with no risk to the orbiter, but Griffin was forced to ground the fleet for another year to further rectify the foam issue. Even though we had come a long way, our team returned to the drawing board to further refine our foam processes.

Griffin was highly challenged with concurrently supporting a 2010 deactivation of the Shuttle Program, completing the International Space Station, and implementing The Vision for Space Exploration. He promptly ordered a study of the exploration systems architecture to shape the goals and determine how best to configure the Constellation program. The result included the development of spacecraft and booster vehicles to replace the Space Shuttle. NASA had already begun designing two boosters, the Ares I and Ares V, utilizing existing Shuttle hardware. Ares I would have had the sole function of launching mission crews into orbit, while Ares V would have been used to launch other hardware for use on missions requiring a heavier lift capacity than the Ares I booster. Griffin referred to the program as "Apollo on steroids."

One year later, STS-121 was preparing for the second Return to Flight mission to test new equipment and procedures to increase Shuttle safety, including the foam on the External Tank, transport supplies, perform maintenance, and deliver a crew member to the Space Station. Griffin was receiving major pushback from many of his NASA colleagues, particularly Safety Officer Bryan O'Connor, due to safety issues with the tank. Griffin weighed the technical data and overruled the concerns. He put together a highly skilled team, and on July 4, 2006, with a spectacular display of sound and light befitting an Independence Day launch, STS-121 thundered off the pad and completed a successful thirteen-day mission. This garnered Griffin immense respect in the space community. It was a true test of his technical and leadership skills.

He followed a similar path when presented with the previous set of parameters for the Hubble Telescope. He assembled a team of program veterans, including former Hubble astronauts Scott Altman, Mike Massimino, and John Grumsfeld, who had supported grounding the mission under the previous administrator.

Once shuttles were flying safely again and repair methods were in place for spacewalking astronauts, Griffin felt confident to run the numbers for the Hubble mission. Based on technical data and the expertise of his team, he made the bold decision to reverse the previous edict to abandon the mission—with one caveat: "I want an experienced crew to train for this mission," he said. John Grumsfeld reversed his support of the previous decision and flew on the successful Hubble mission along with Scott Altman, Mike Massimino, and four rookie astronauts.

NASA determined that the new safety modifications, post-Columbia, would make it safer to travel to Hubble. The science community was elated knowing that the repair mission was valuable enough to merit the risk and thereby increasing its life span by ten years. There would be a "launch on need" on the pad at KSC, a scanning process to view any damage to the orbiter in flight, an extravehicular repair capability, and an experienced and willing crew ready to go. When I learned of the decision to return to Hubble for repairs, I was excited and encouraged to know that NASA was, once again, realizing the importance of taking risks and reaching out farther. My respect for Mike Griffin was reinforced by this decision. It was a glimmer of the "old" NASA, a bold move indeed and ultimately one of Griffin's finest moments. The upgrades to the Shuttle after the Columbia accident made it possible to launch the highly successful STS-125 mission to repair the ailing Hubble Space Telescope, which is currently returning greater science than we ever dreamed possible.

Mission Success Bulletin: Final Hubble Mission a Success

STS-125 crewmembers autographing Hubble-
themed Shuttle Model. Courtesy NASA

I first met Mike Griffin several years after the Hubble repair
mission during an event where I was displaying my artwork
at the Space and Rocket Center in Huntsville. It was the first
time he had seen my artwork and he was so impressed that he
stopped by my table later that evening to commission me to
build a Shuttle model for him. I sent him periodic pictures of
the progress of his model, and over the next year, I developed
a friendly relationship with him. He graciously shared his time
with me and became a valued resource for this book, particularly
regarding his involvement with Return to Flight STS-114,
STS-121, and the Hubble Telescope. I believe that if the 2008
presidential election had turned out differently, he would have
continued in his position as the NASA administrator, and our
space program would have taken a much different course.

He is a true leader and visionary who continues to hold great
hope for the future of our manned space program. He embraced
the challenges of the position, but expressed disappointment in the
underlying political climate, especially during Hurricane Katrina,
when political forces lobbied him to relocate the Michoud facility

to their respective states. He felt a strong allegiance to the team in New Orleans and had no intention of abandoning Michoud.

Approximately four months after the Columbia accident, Jim Kennedy was propelled into the position of director at KSC. He later e-mailed me, saying, "I kept the Shuttle model you made for me at MSFC in my office during the Columbia Accident Investigation, and it served as a treasured and inspirational piece during that difficult and challenging time."

This has been both a personal and painful recollection of my journey of overwhelming grief, love, and authentic passion. Amazingly, they all crescendoed to a peak with the mind-blowing pictures that we have received from Hubble Telescope. I believe it is the closest we will ever come to heaven on earth.

Eagle Nebula

Eagle Nebula. Courtesy NASA

Cat's Eye Nebula

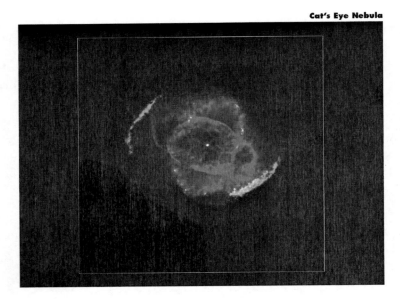

Cat's Eye Nebula. Courtesy NASA

Woodism

The human spirit trumps adversity.

Katrina and Our
Modern-Day Cowboys

Return to Flight, STS-114, had barely landed when, on August 29, 2005, the Gulf Coast was hit with powerful Category 5 Hurricane Katrina. While the nation was focused on the chaos and human toll in the New Orleans area and along the Mississippi Gulf Coast, America's manned space flight program was also in major jeopardy, including the Michoud Assembly Facility and nearby Stennis Space Center in Bay St. Louis, with more than 7,000 NASA and contractor personnel affected. As part of our contingency plan, a ride-out team of thirty-eight Lockheed Martin and NASA employees volunteered to hunker down inside the Michoud Facility to protect valuable space flight hardware where the External Tanks were built, processed, and stored.

As the storm battered the huge 400+ acre Michoud complex, the team kept generators running and storm drainage pumps operating. The interior of the tank production building stayed dry as winds assaulted the heavy steel doors. The water rose six inches around the facility, and several buildings suffered window and roof damage. One tank, ET-122, was deemed unusable after a concrete roof panel fell and bounced off its side.

Roof damage on Vehicle Assembly Building at Michoud post Katrina. Courtesy NASA

Mission Success Bulletin Artifact

The facility avoided catastrophic damage, but we suffered one indirect fatality. A former supervisor and a friend from the Mudman days, at age fifty-two, succumbed to a heart attack during the storm as a result of not receiving timely emergency medical treatment. He left behind a wife and daughter and a huge hole in our Quality Control Department.

Even after the storm passed, land routes were cut off, and the facility was without electricity and water for twenty-one days. Within hours after the storm hit, the team at MSFC realized the devastation and mobilized our contingency plan to gather building supplies, construction tools, food, bottled water, medicines and first aid, personal items, and clothing. I boxed up the supplies and loaded them on a NASA aircraft for transport to the recovery workers trying to restore communications and power at the Michoud facility. Because all systems were shut down in New Orleans, the only credit-card authority was in the hands of a few of us at MSFC. We arranged for the urgent supplies to be transported by helicopter, which was the only way in while land routes were cut off.

Short-term housing was provided to employees while they heroically worked to restore the facility, bringing it back online to accept two tanks from KSC for processing and retrofitting to correct foam issues discovered during the STS-114 mission the previous month. NASA Administrator Mike Griffin later said, "It's not about money or holding a job. It's about dedication to the program—dedication money can't buy."

Several of the test facilities were partially flooded, and more than half of our employees had sustained significant personal loss, including to homes and cars. To their relief, the NASA contracting officer at MSFC found a clause in the ET contract that stated the government would continue to pay contract employees if, due to no fault of their own, the facility was shut down. Their paychecks were direct deposited, and they did not lose any pay as a result of Katrina. This served to buoy a group that was already devastated emotionally, physically, and financially. Kudos to NASA! New Orleans was devastated by Katrina, but our work on the External Tank did not stop. We were not going to let a category 5 hurricane deter us from meeting our schedule of the second Return to Flight, STS-121.

New Orleans devastated by Hurricane Katrina

Not only was I continuing to support the foam modifications with an already short-staffed office, but I was also thrust into the middle of supporting the Katrina relief effort. After several hundred employees were temporarily relocated to Huntsville from the Michoud facility, I was provided with additional personnel. I was finally in a position to delegate minor tasks so that I could appropriately support the onslaught of temporary personnel with supplies and transportation needs.

During each hurricane season, we reviewed our contingency plan for the External Tank Program at Michoud with the knowledge that critical commodities—such as refrigerated foam insulation, precious metals, primers, and long-lead items—had to be protected and moved out of the way of a storm. The plan was to load them onto trucks prior to a storm and moved 400 miles to a safe zone. With the hurricane on its way, our contingency plan kicked into action, and we were able to remove the items before Katrina hit. Dozens of trucks were loaded with precious cargo from New Orleans and headed to Huntsville for safe haven until the waters receded and it was safe to reenter the Michoud facility.

Over my thirty years with the Space Shuttle Program, I had the pleasure of working with many truck drivers who delivered our flight hardware with the care of a parent for his child. These were independent drivers with limited loads, drop trailers, flatbeds, oversized loads, as well as Federal Express and UPS drivers. Some were corporate, and some were mom-and-pop partnerships.

As a kid, I thought of truck drivers as rather rough and tumble, like cowboys roaming the range. In my professional life, I found them always hungry for the latest information about what was going on in the space program and for details about the loads they were carrying. Whenever I stopped by the NASA Public Affairs office, I always picked up lithographs, patches, and posters to have on hand for when the truck drivers stopped by. I knew they would be thrilled to have some precious space memorabilia to carry back to their children and grandchildren.

I was responsible for coordinating itineraries and keeping the truck drivers informed of scheduling while they were in the "holding pattern" during the Katrina relocation. I saw how the life of an independent driver could be monotonous and lonely. The truck becomes a temporary home. I felt it was important to let them know they were part of our mission. I made a special effort to spend time with them for the two to three months they spent at truck stops in and around Marshall Space Flight Center. I would periodically stop by to share space program mementos and information. By the time they were given the go-ahead to return to New Orleans, I was sure they had picked up an enthusiasm for our mission and would play a part in spreading the word.

Scott with trucks in "holding pattern" at
MSFC during Hurricane Katrina

Kudos to all the truck drivers—our modern-day cowboys—who got through during Katrina and enabled the space program to get back to operation quickly and efficiently to complete the External Tanks in New Orleans!

Woodism

Tell somebody about the space program and they will forget. Ask them about the space program and they may remember. Give them something tangible and they will understand.

Preparing for an Unknown Future

After we successfully completed the Return to Flight of the Shuttle, our team was still in denial about the planned retirement of our world-class Space Shuttle Program. Yet we were also apprehensively excited about the new vision to go back to the moon.

When President Bush revealed the vision early in 2004, we were given six years to get the Shuttle flying again, finish the missions, and navigate a smooth transition between closing out the thirty-year program and gearing up for the next challenge, a two-rocket system known as Constellation. We were motivated and excited about the new program, which would introduce Ares I, a heritage Shuttle solid-rocket booster with a capsule named Orion to carry the crew, and Ares V, a cargo carrier utilizing heritage Shuttle hardware and employing the skill sets of existing workers. We could see the merits of the new program, and we were willing to trade the Space Shuttle for this ambitious new vision.

Huntsville Times artifact outlining the transition
from Shuttle to Constellation Program

While my team was focused on STS-114 Return to Flight, NASA, for one of the final planned missions, agreed to upgrade and repair the ET-122 tank that had been damaged during Katrina in 2005. This prolonged hundreds of jobs pending layoff due to the decreased production of External Tanks after the Columbia accident. NASA sanctioned an idea to design a special logo for the ET-122 to honor all the workers who knew they would receive a pink slip after the upgrades and repairs were completed yet diligently maintained their high level of detail and craftsmanship. The design, which depicted a Shuttle flying through the eye of a hurricane was painted on the intertank door. When it successfully launched into orbit on Endeavour's final mission, STS-134, in May 2011, the logo was on the back of the tank. I felt pride as well as sadness for the losses from both Katrina and the job cuts.

ET-122 intertank door with special logo

A year passed after Bush's announcement with business as usual and no clear transition to the new Constellation program. The long hours spent getting the Shuttle flying again temporarily distracted us from the worry of how we were going to make the changeover and where we would fit into the plan. We continued with the mind-set that the Shuttle would not be eliminated until a new system was perfected. We didn't realize we were in the midst of the best of times and the worst of times.

One day, a question crossed my mind: Would they possibly discontinue the Shuttle before a replacement was ready? Surely, they wouldn't let go of all the highly skilled workers and loyal vendors, especially considering our country was in the midst of the worst economic downturn in seventy years.

After launching STS-114 Return to Flight in the summer of 2005, we started to witness partisan bickering in Congress, and with the distraction of the Iraqi war, President Bush showed a lack of attention to domestic issues, including the Space Program. The vision of returning to the moon was not communicated to the American public.

Bush visited Huntsville on June 2, 2007, the day before STS-117 returned from a fourteen-day mission. But rather than make a four-mile trip to MSFC, the president traveled thirty miles from the Huntsville airport for a brief speech at the Tennessee Valley Authority nuclear facility, which had recently been brought back online after being shut down for two decades due to safety issues. I was perplexed. It seemed like the president had missed a perfect opportunity to bask in a JFK-type moment, proclaiming that we would return to the moon. A few positive words from him during that time would have provided a desperately needed morale boost. I felt it was a missed opportunity. The press also failed to seize the moment. No mention was made of the very thing that put their community on the map in "Rocket City."

As I continued to reflect on that protocol decision, I was struck with the overwhelming feeling that perhaps the future of our manned space flight program might not be the priority we thought. We had only been willing to accept the Shuttle's demise without protest when we believed there was a better program to follow.

Contemplating the worst-case scenario, I wrote down my predictions for the future of our manned space flight program:

1. The administration would let go of the Shuttle and thousands of capable vendors and skilled workers.
2. We would begin to pay the Russians hundreds of millions of dollars to transport our astronauts to the space station.
3. America would no longer be in the manned space flight business, and we would lose most of our astronaut corps after spending millions of dollars training them.

4. Our industrial base, shared with the military, would suffer.
5. Hydrogen production in the United States would be severely cut when no longer required for the Shuttle.
6. Local economies would suffer collateral damage with the loss of secondary services.
7. The American pride and leadership role we held for our space program and the encouragement for the next generation would be gravely diminished.

Our world-class manned space flight program, billions of dollars, and the livelihood of tens of thousands of skilled workers were potentially headed over a cliff. And all of this would happen for a mere 7/10 of 1 percent of our nation's expenditure—NASA's annual budget.

As the Shuttle program wound down and contracts were awarded for the Constellation Program, we continued to do our jobs. We successfully returned the Shuttle to flight, and we produced the External Tanks that would let NASA complete the assembly of the International Space Station.

In the fall of 2008, President-Elect Obama sent Lori Garver, a former adviser on his presidential campaign, to meet with NASA Administrator Mike Griffin to be briefed on the Constellation Program. She informed NASA that the new administration would "look under the hood" before signing on to the new moon program. What we believed was a viable program, was now in jeopardy.

Soon after he was sworn into office, President Obama commissioned a ten-member blue-ribbon panel of astronauts, academics, and private industry representatives, headed by Norman Augustine, an esteemed former executive with Lockheed Martin. The stated goal was to ensure that the nation was on "a vigorous and sustainable path to achieving its boldest aspirations in space." The committee began work in June 2009 with a six-month time frame and a budget of $3 million.

e Huntsville Times

13, 2009   We break news online   Visit our Web site at al.com   **Classifieds 532-4222**

Ares may be in jeopardy

White House panel considers extending shuttle program

By Shelby G. Spires
Times Aerospace Writer
shelby.spires@htimes.com

The Ares I rocket, managed at Marshall Space Flight Center, might become a museum piece before it ever blasts off on a mission if a White House-appointed panel discussion Wednesday is any indication about NASA's future.

The committee was a major topic of discussion, and one option deems the whole Constellation program – a space shuttle replacement and moon effort NASA has been working on for almost five years – as too expensive for the space agency's $18 billion budget.

NASA has spent $3 billion over the past four years to develop Ares I, which would be used to loft astronauts to the International Space Station or be used with the much larger Ares V on a moon mission.

During its final planned public meeting in Washington, D.C., the Augustine Commission reviewed several options for NASA's future, including extending the space shuttle to 2015, using the space station until 2020 and sending humans to asteroids using a variant of the larger Ares V rocket.

Missions to Mars also took

a back seat because "we think Mars direct (flight) is not a mission we are prepared to take on technically or financially," said aerospace veteran Norman Augustine, panel chair.

The bulk of the Ares I mission, at the end of the next decade, would be to fly as-

See ARES on A7

Huntsville Times artifact dated August 13, 2009

As an avid student of space policy, I believe the Augustine Committee was provided with highly unrealistic guidelines from the Office of Management and Budget (OMB). The budget furnished was lower than the one offered by the Bush Administration and the committee reached the conclusion that there would not be enough money to allow Americans to return to the moon before the late 2020s. I don't fault the committee; I fault the guidelines they were given. Anyone confronted with the logic they received would have reached the same conclusions. The committee actually recommended that the Obama Administration add about $3 billion per year to NASA's budget. I considered that a drop in the bucket considering our space program was the heart and soul of the leadership in space.

Four months later, in October 2009, the committee concluded that because the multi-billion-dollar Constellation Program was so far behind schedule, underfunded, and over budget, they determined that meeting any of its goals would not be possible.

Huntsville Times

2009   We break news online Visit our Web site at al.com   Classifieds 532-4222

OCT 23, 2009

» The Augustine Report   *LeT MAE BAttle Begin*

Cancel Ares I, panel says

Alabama lawmakers criticize report on direction of NASA

By Shelby G. Spires
Times Aerospace Writer
shelby.spires@htimes.com

Members of the Alabama congressional delegation Thursday were swift to criticize a report that may set the course of NASA, Marshall

More Online
Read the full report at
www.al.com/boost

Space Flight Center and its Ares rocket program for years to come.

Sent to the White House late Wednesday, the 155-page Augustine Commission study recommends canceling the Ares I rocket managed at

Marshall Space Flight Center and moving on to the heavy-lift Ares V, awarding rocket launches to contractors, and sending astronauts to nearby asteroids. The report was sent to members of Congress early Thursday.

"America is the richest nation in the world," U.S. Rep. Parker Griffith, D-Huntsville, told *The Times* by phone. "We can bail out to the tune of almost $1 trillion; we can find

NASA more money. The world expects us to lead, and NASA is the heart and soul of leadership in space."

The report held no surprises or changes from a summary released earlier to the public, said former Lockheed CEO Norman Augustine, who chaired the commission over its five months of work.

Options suggested in the report all count on NASA get-

ting at least $3 billion more a year over the next decade. The report suggests putting the money toward supporting science on the International Space Station and developing the Marshall-managed Ares V large cargo rocket.

"The human space flight program the United States is currently pursuing is one on an unsustainable trajectory,"

See ARES on A7

Huntsville Times artifact

Based on these findings, Obama zeroed out the Constellation Program from his 2010 budget and pulled the plug on the vision of going back to the moon. Shortly thereafter, an initial $1.6 billion a year was diverted to commercial rocket endeavors, primarily Space Exploration Technologies Corporation (SpaceX), to develop a rocket system that could carry cargo and eventually crews to the International Space Station (ISS), and millions of dollars were transferred to the Russians, who would provide our only access to the ISS.

JAN 28, 2010

Anxiety rises over NASA budget

Space experts say wait to see actual numbers before panicking

By Lee Roop
Times Staff Writer
lee.roop@htimes.com

Anxiety about the future of manned space flight – and 2,200

local jobs – is building amid reports that President Barack Obama will propose a 2011 NASA budget Monday that weakens or kills the Constellation program.

"President Obama's decision, if it is indeed to be as is rumored today, leaves NASA and the nation with no program, no plan, and no commitment to any human spaceflight program be-

In today's *Times*
Dr. Mike Griffin's statement. A8

yond that of today – the last few flights of the space shuttle to complete the International Space Station," Dr. Mike Griffin, former NASA administrator and now eminent scholar at the University of Alabama in Huntsville, said

Wednesday.

"I've read what you've read," said Steve Cook, who ran the Ares rocket component of Constellation at Marshall Space Flight Center from conception until leaving for a job in industry in September.

"This is just a lot of speculation,"

See NASA on A8

Dr. Mike Griffin, former NASA chief

Huntsville Times artifact dated

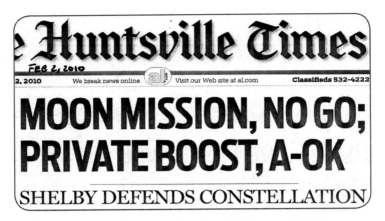

Huntsville Times

FEB 2, 2010

2, 2010   We break news online   al   Visit our Web site at al.com   **Classifieds 532-4222**

MOON MISSION, NO GO; PRIVATE BOOST, A-OK

SHELBY DEFENDS CONSTELLATION

Huntsville Times artifact dated February 2, 2010

For several years, we had labored on a dying program, believing that we were gearing up for an ambitious new vision. Our hope was turned to anguish, and the American public was kept in the dark as their manned space program was being destroyed. Letters signed by sixty-two esteemed House members, both Democratic and Republican; Senators John McCain, Kay Bailey Hutchison, and David Vitter; and former astronauts Scott Carpenter, Gene Cernan, and Charlie Duke were written to Obama urging him to extend the Space Shuttle program until we had a clear path to alternative launch capabilities. As a result of the political pressure, two additional flights were added to fly equipment to finish the International Space Station. It was a small reprieve but only a temporary one.

For the first time in NASA's fifty-year history, they did not have a follow-on program. Shuttle Launch Director, Mike Leinback, voiced it this way, "Throughout the history of the manned space flight program we've always had another program to transition into—from Mercury to Gemini, and to Apollo and the Apollo-Soyuz test program, to Skylab and then to the Shuttle." Without the new Constellation Program to transition to, not only was the entire Shuttle Program being shut down, but valuable assets and critical skill sets would be lost, and we would lose the momentum for future endeavors. The Shuttle Orbiters were eviscerated and placed in museums, and the infrastructure—including launch pads and facilities—was either torn down or decommissioned. The only American access to orbit was deactivated before we had a replacement system, essentially giving Russia the keys to the International Space Station.

Shuttle Orbiters gutted. Courtesy NASA

Skyrocketing inflation: Russia now charging NASA $70 million per seat to fly US astronauts

Published April 30, 2013

March 28, 2013: A Russian Soyuz rocket blasts off from the Central Asian spaceport of Baikonur Cosmodrome in Kazakhstan carrying a new crew to the International Space Station. NASA

Those of us who had given the Shuttle program our love and our lives for so many years were powerless to do anything as we watched it being killed, and worse, we were now being told to help destroy it.

As a logistics engineer, I liked a quote by General Norman Schwarzkopf, who said, "Armchair generals study tactics. Real generals study logistics." One of the first lessons we learn in a huge program like the Shuttle is to pay attention to the details of supplies, vendors, and parts manufacturers. That will determine the success or the failure of an operation more than anything else that management does.

I began the agonizing task of calling long-standing vendors—many mom-pop companies—with the devastating news, knowing it would mean that they would be forced to close their doors. Many or most of our orders were not ordinary products. We were the only buyer for many items. When we stopped buying them, they would stop being produced. The production equipment would be disposed of. It would become impossible to ever just change our mind and say, "Send us another batch." With every call I had to make, I was driving another nail into the coffin of the Space Shuttle.

Despite the pain of the transition, NASA had to complete the job of finishing the Space Station and ending the Space Shuttle Program. It needed to keep the workers necessary to finish that job, even though those might see the necessity of using the time before their impending layoffs to look for more stable employment. The Space Shuttle had a large workforce in the region, and particularly during the difficult economy of the time, there would not be enough jobs for everyone who was facing eventual layoff. What reason would workers have to stay on the program while the limited outside jobs were being filled by the people who left the program first?

During the remaining flights of the Shuttle program, NASA approved a payout incentive program for prime contractors to motivate key employees to continue on the program through the conclusion of their individual work scope. The External Tank plan was based on a successful incentive process used by Lockheed Martin at the end of the Titan Intercontinental Ballistic Missile Program model in 2005.

Starting with STS-124 in May 2008, an account was created for each key employee with an initial base incentive amount and payments for each tank delivery and successful launch/landing milestones were added to employee accounts. These financial incentives, however, were contingent upon our working until our individual end dates. If you resigned or were let go for cause prior to your completion date, you forfeited your incentive, leaving the program with nothing. It was a coercive tool with little concern for the human toll.

Whenever the manifest was updated or there were significant changes to the program, we were invited to status meetings, where letters were distributed informing on who would be extended. At every meeting, there were always four or five coworkers who received an early completion date. It was always apparent who received a new end date by the frozen stares on their faces. For the next couple of months, those who were transitioning out became almost invisible during staff meetings as their input was diminished. They were known as dead men walking. It was brutal. And everyone knew that he or she could be the next on the chopping block. It wore on the mind—and on the nerves. This happened to me six times over the last two years of the program. But I prayed that I would be one of the last people out. My goal was to finish what I started with STS-1.

Whenever someone received their completion date, they were forced to cross-train coworkers prior to their departure in order to receive their payout. Those who remained often felt survivor's guilt as they siphoned information from those leaving. It became a viciously competitive environment. People got downright venomous; it was personal.

Two of my colleagues were close personal friends—their families literally grew up together—in addition to working closely together for more than twenty years. But when they learned that their manager was faced with making a choice between them, one revealed that the other had been placing personal business on his computer. He had looked the other way for years until it became his ticket to continued employment.

As people left the program, their work shifted to others. You were expected to adjust to the added workload or face losing your incentive. My job was "one of one," meaning I had no backup, and so taking vacation time was practically out of the question. In Logistics, you cannot let any of the balls drop.

Every day was like walking on a tightrope. We counted down—three years...two years...one year. Then it became month-to-month, day-to-day. It was inevitable. One by one, my friends and colleagues were discarded like baggage that was no longer needed. I knew my time would come as well.

Our team was like a "tribe." Initially, we were developing our credibility and expertise, and we had minimal influence toward the mission. It took years to perfect our skills, and when we realized our ideas and expertise were beginning to be valued, we felt like the mission depended on our specialized skills. By the end of the program, we had reached the highest level of expertise.

It was heartbreaking to watch my tribe be disassembled, and it was heartbreaking to watch these people leave, people who had worked so hard on every single mission. Our team had been together so long, and each of us had experienced each tribal level, individually and as a team. We had developed effective communication, trust, and a high level of skill. We were a team working in the same direction with shared values and common goals. We were at the top of our craft.

Losing a tribe like that is a double loss. There's the loss of people you've toiled alongside for years. That is heartbreaking enough. But the respect and credibility you achieved was given by people who knew you and your work. I watched these people leave, knowing they may also be losing hard-earned respect for their experience and accomplishments.

With the world watching, our team successfully resolved the issue with the ECO sensors that were prohibiting STS-122 from flying. It was because of our collective knowledge and skill that we were successful in making the necessary repairs. Based on the exclusive work of our team, NASA had the confidence that we had resolved the ECO sensor issue and made the final decision to launch STS-122. And together, with NASA, we moved forward with the final successful thirteen Shuttle flights.

In mid-2009, a "stop-order" for new External Tank production was issued. That was the final nail. Any hope of going beyond the thirteen flights was over. With no program to transition to, the thought of starting over in a poor economy was insurmountable to many people. Some retired, many faced layoffs, others drank or flipped out emotionally. Several even committed suicide. Sadly, one worker jumped from launch pad 39-A at KSC. Endeavour was on the pad in March 2011 when it happened, getting ready for her last launch two months later. An engineer who worked on the pad's swing arm who had recently gotten his layoff notice jumped 130 feet from the tower to the pad below. He had a note in his wallet to his wife and children, saying that he did not want to be a burden on them. The man was a contractor with United Space Alliance, which laid off about 2,800 highly skilled people at the end of the program.

The situation was also particularly harsh at Michoud in New Orleans. Many of our coworkers were still recovering from losing their homes as a result of Katrina, and now, they were faced with losing their livelihoods. It was a heart-breaking and demoralizing situation.

While I still had my job for the moment, the uncertainty and change affecting the Shuttle workforce was definitely taking a toll on me. In addition to not knowing how much longer I would be at the job, I did not know what would come next. What would replace my income, and what would our lives look like without it? I had been with the program since before the first launch, and among people at NASA, I was known as "Shuttleman." What would happen to "Shuttleman" when there was no more Shuttle? This was more than a job, more than a mission; it was a passion, and it had become part of my identity. What happens when you lose a large piece of who you are? After you've worked on one of the most incredible programs in the history of our country, most other jobs pale in comparison. There was no going back to the early levels of a tribe for me. I would have to create a plan.

One day, I found inspiration in a random way. I normally worked through lunch, and often, as a small diversion, I would seek out a new word on the computer and play with it until it became part of my vocabulary. I was quite intrigued the day I found the Japanese word *gaman*. The word's introduction to America has been attributed to the more than 100,000 Japanese-Americans who were held in US internment camps during World War II. The "gaman spirit" came to describe the ability to do your best during distressed times and maintain self-control and discipline. Taking that one step further, the "art of gaman" is the ability to turn something negative into something positive. *Gaman* became my inspiration and served as a springboard going forward.

Given the political climate, I realized that our space program would be in disarray for many years. That, combined with the disappointments I heard from friend after friend, put me into action to make some serious decisions about my future. Returning to my childhood inspiration, I needed to be involved in something larger than me and something that would make a difference to mankind...things that included a legacy. Until the day when space exploration, once again, is at the forefront of our country's priorities, I would have to change my paradigm and forge a new path for my future.

On my fiftieth birthday, February 12, 2009, I was surprised with a Vision Day®, a retreat focused on personal strategic planning and renewing my direction in life, hosted by two amazing executive coaches—my sister Deb and her husband, Rob. The theme of my Vision Day was "Preparing for an Unknown Future." We developed a formal two-year plan that would engage my creativity and occupy my thoughts during an otherwise stressful time.

My bucket list consisted of five things that would have long-lasting value:

1. Organize Shuttle library and memorabilia into a world-class collection;
2. Build a lasting tangible tribute to the Space Shuttle Program;
3. Accomplish my lifelong dream of owning a custom-built HD28 Martin guitar with a Shuttle inlay;
4. Travel to the last Shuttle launch with my family and gain access to the pad; and
5. Write a memoir chronicling my thirty-plus years on the Space Shuttle Program.

I felt empowered.

Woodism

Change is inevitable. A wise person will be ready.

Be Your Best…at Your Worst

Given the short and unpredictable timeframe of the program shutdown and the enormity of my vision, I had to be focused and proactive in moving ahead with my plans. I worried about how I could maintain my enthusiasm for a program that had received a death sentence, but I trusted in my gut that I would find a silver lining and carve out a new path using the heritage of the Shuttle Program to create possibilities for my future. I would draw on my strengths and past successes with my extensive memorabilia collection, firsthand stories, one-of-a-kind art pieces, and the connections I had developed to accomplish my bucket list.

My tribute project began in mid-2009, two years before the Space Shuttle Program actually ended after 135 missions. Having a limited time to accomplish my goals gave me a boldness I might not otherwise have had. Bringing others into this project, more than anything else, helped me through the losses, and I was inspired to write a formal proposal to the MSFC Shuttle Projects Team headed by Director Steven Cash. It included details of a tribute incorporating a couple of small pieces of wood autographed by former President Jimmy Carter, a world-class woodworker. When Carter retired from office, his staff wanted to present him with a new car, but he vetoed the idea. Instead, they sent him off with tools and equipment to outfit his workshop in Plains, Georgia, where he continues to build unique furniture pieces that are auctioned off to benefit the Carter Center, a nonprofit organization that funds his philanthropic endeavors. He had recently built a six-foot persimmon cabinet that sold for more than $1 million.

Carter had been president during the development phase of the Shuttle Program, and so it seemed a natural fit that we could obtain a few autographed scraps from his workshop to incorporate into the Shuttle Tribute. His signature would be used as authentication for local and national press. NASA was excited about my idea, and we secured the approval of top management of the Shuttle Program, John Shannon and Wayne Hale, to fly wood pieces from Carter's workshop on the Shuttle. They would then be returned to me and placed in the tribute to honor Carter's contributions. The project would be a win-win for everyone involved: The Shuttle Team would be presented with a one-of-a-kind tribute to the Shuttle Program to honor their work, President Carter would receive positive press for his contributions, and I would have a project to direct my energies. Several months later, I received the green light from management to fly wood from President Carter into space. While I was concurrently getting that project underway and collecting flight pins commemorating the various flights, I started a bingo-type sheet of Shuttle missions and invited the Shuttle team to participate in the tribute by contributing mission pins for specific flights that had significance to them and writing their names next to them. My initial effort to contact President Carter was a call to Tony Clark, the press secretary of the Carter Library and a former CNN reporter. He loved the plan and forwarded the request to the Carter Center. Three days later, NASA followed up with a formal letter to President Carter requesting his participation in the tribute. We were all confident that he would agree, but surprisingly, on the same day, we received an e-mail from Carter's office respectfully turning down our request. I was stunned. There was no explanation, just a flat-out no. I thought this was merely a standard form letter in response to my verbal request, and perhaps he had not actually received the formal letter from NASA. Through a personal connection, however, I learned that NASA's request had, in fact, been brought to Carter's attention, and the decision stood. I was angry; it just didn't seem right. What harm would there have been to pick up a couple scraps of wood out of his workshop trash bin? I felt a sense of betrayal knowing this could have been an all-around win-win situation.

In trying to understand Carter's decision, I did some research and discovered that he had contributed very little to the overall Shuttle Program, which was started during the Nixon era. In fact, Carter reduced the hardware, including canceling a planned fifth Orbiter. At the same time, he opened the door to military exploitation in space supporting future development of anti-satellite technologies. Had it not been for the fact that the Soviets seemed intimidated by the Shuttle, the program might not have survived his presidency. Even if he had been initially indifferent to the program, the Shuttle had earned its place in history with the payloads, the incredible science and medical breakthroughs, the Hubble Space Telescope, and the collaboration with thirteen nations on the International Space Station. For decades, it had motivated millions of people around the world. It was disheartening to know that fourteen astronauts had perished, and yet Carter was unwilling to participate in honoring the program legacy. I may have escorted his wife back in the day, but I had no idea of his lack of support for the manned space flight program. I realized it had been a major mistake to try to include him. With that opportunity closed, I had to explore other avenues.

While recovering from this setback, I came across an article announcing that C. F. Martin Guitar, one of America's oldest companies, was celebrating its 175th anniversary. In their timeline for 1994, it listed "the first American guitar flown in space" exhibit. In 1994, as Launch Honoree, Dianne and I had traveled to the STS-62 launch, which coincidentally, was the mission that flew the Martin guitar in space. While reminiscing about playing "Country Roads" on my vintage Martin guitar in the External Tank, I thought about the connection Martin Guitar had with wood and their collaboration with NASA in the past. I got an idea about placing one of my Shuttle art pieces in the C. F. Martin Museum, along with the first American guitar flown in space. Added to my goal of owning a Martin guitar, this felt like a sign or perhaps a divine intervention. It gave me the confidence to contact the company to solicit their partnership on the project. And I could order my HD28 at the same time!

I began my relationship with C. F. Martin Guitar Company in the summer of 2009. I was sitting at my desk during lunch and thought, *What the heck*. I picked up the phone and called their headquarters in Nazareth, Pennsylvania. Dick Boak answered, and after I introduced myself, I enthusiastically told him about my idea. To my good fortune, it turned out that Boak was C. F. Martin's artist, public relations, and museum curator. He embraced the idea of placing one of my models in the museum, and so began the journey. Over the next year or so, I shared my vision for the model with Boak, and he graciously sent several pieces of wood to be used in the tribute, including ebony cutoffs from a D12 guitar that Martin was crafting for singer/songwriter David Crosby, and some Brazilian rosewood out of his personal collection.

The Shuttle model I crafted for the museum, Serial #10-15, was finished in January 2011. I used the Crosby ebony to make the external tank nose cone and the Brazilian rosewood in the body of the orbiter. Because C. F. Martin Guitar Company is located on Sycamore Street, I used sycamore wood for the three main engines. To further connect my woodworking with guitars, after I write a song, I remove the guitar strings and use them as my burnishing tool on the Shuttle's tank and boosters. Like Martin guitars, all my models receive a serial number to document the date it was made and the traceability of its heritage.

With great anticipation, I arrived at the C. F. Martin Guitar Company in Nazareth, Pennsylvania, on January 19, 2011. I was announced, and within minutes, Dick Boak came down to meet me. He had cleared his calendar to spend the entire day with me. We proceeded through an electronic entrance upstairs to the executive suite. After stopping for a cup of coffee, we went to his office, where the boxes of NASA promotional items and the Shuttle model I sent ahead of time were waiting. I hoped there would be an opportunity to meet Chris Martin, the sixth-generation owner of C. F. Martin. So I was blown away when Boak informed me that Mr. Martin wanted to meet me and that we would unveil the Shuttle model with him, in his office. Martin loved the model and inquired about the LOX feed line and commented on how much he enjoyed the level of detail. It was a bittersweet meeting as his younger brother had passed away the day before I arrived.

Boak and I carried the Shuttle model to the museum. He unlocked the glass case and placed the model next to the first American guitar in space. He allowed me to handle the guitar that Astronaut Pierre Thuot carried into space on STS-62, which was a great thrill.

After lunch, Boak took me on a private tour of the guitar factory. I felt like a movie star. I visited one-on-one with the craftspeople, and we presented them with Shuttle lithographs and NASA "meatball" logo stickers along the way. I felt proud to be an American as I watched these world-class artisans working and experienced the authenticity exhibited by this extraordinary company.

Knowing that I am passionate about history, Boak invited me into their archive vault, which was quite obviously not part of the general tour. What an honor that was! They had huge volumes of sales ledgers going back to the early 1900s as well as letters from many famous people, including Elvis Presley and Gene Autry. It was both fascinating and highly informative.

My moment had come. Boak asked me, "Are you ready to see it?" We went back to his office, and I was presented with my new HD28 guitar. It unequivocally exceeded my expectations. The inlay, crafted by artist, Tracy Cox, depicting the STS-1 Shuttle launching off the pad was stunning! We took lots of pictures, including one interesting shot of me holding my guitar in front of a picture of C. F. Martin III holding a guitar in the same fashion. All I could think was, "Wow!"

When my amazing day came to an end, I felt a real connection. I left part of my family—my Shuttle model—with them, and felt that I would forever be a part of the Martin family. I had always loved the rich heritage of C. F. Martin Company, and now I understood why I had felt a kindred spirit toward them. I also could check off another item on my bucket list—my HD28 Martin guitar!

Part of my inspiration for the tribute had been to include Space Shuttle team members in the project as a way of easing their pain as well and staying connected. Most people were very supportive and understood what I was trying to do. Among my supporters was Jeremy Kelly, who worked at Lockheed Martin's Hot Gas Facility. His family manufactured wood cabinets, and he worked with them part-time. I enlisted his help in making the walnut box I had designed that would be the base for the tribute. The finished product was executed brilliantly to my exact specifications. Kelly was so honored to be part of the project that he delivered it gratis. Another contribution to the project was provided by NASA employee Michael Suits. He acquired the final flight pin, carried it to the last launch, STS-135, and then installed it as the final piece on the tribute. There were many more who understood what I was trying to accomplish and encouraged me along the journey. More than 100 key people supported the project by autographing the back, taking it even beyond what I had envisioned.

MARTIN STORIES *MARTIN STORIES* **MARTIN STORIES** *MARTIN STORIES* **MARTIN STORIES** *MARTIN S*

NASA's Scott Phillips

Scott "Shuttleman" Phillips works at NASA's Marshall Space Flight Center in Huntsville, Alabama. He's a Logistics Engineer for Lockheed Martin on the Space Shuttle's external tank program. As an avid woodworker, Scott was inspired early on in his career with the space program to create exotic wood models of many (if not all) of the shuttle flights. He is also a singer, songwriter and guitarist with a deep love for Martin guitars.

As the final shuttle mission approached, Scott contacted Martin to see if there might be some special pieces of Martin wood appropriate for his last model. Martin's Dick Boak furnished Scott with some special cutoffs, including a piece of ebony from David Crosby's one-of-a-kind 12-string with an ebony neck. This piece became the nose cone for the model above, that Scott very generously donated for display in the Martin Museum. It resides next to the McNally-Martin Space Guitar that was the first guitar to orbit the earth on a shuttle mission.

Scott also commissioned a unique HD-28 Martin guitar that bears a specially inlaid NASA-themed pickguard by inlay artist Tracy Cox. To top it off, astronaut John Glenn and Chris Martin signed the interior label for Scott's guitar. Scott's visited Martin recently to deliver his model and to pick up his guitar. It was an emotional and meaningful day for Scott and for everyone at Martin who met him.

Scott Phillips, above, with his special NASA-inspired Martin guitar. Below, during the installation of his shuttle model in the Martin Museum, Scott got to sample the Space Guitar that accompanied astronaut/mission specialist/guitarist Pierre Thuot aboard space shuttle Columbia that launched on March 4, 1994. Of course the mission was: "To Boldly Go Where No Guitar Has Gone Before!"

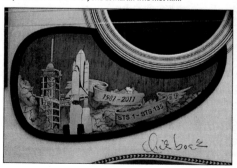

5

C.F. Martin's bi-annual magazine, Sounding Board,
with feature article dated July 2011

The tribute began to take on a life of its own. For the thirtieth anniversary of the Space Shuttle Program, NASA requested that the tribute be displayed at MSFC headquarters. The tribute turned out to be the focal commemorative piece at MSFC honoring the thirty-year milestone. The astronaut crews who flew on the final flights of the three orbiters, Discovery, Atlantis, and Endeavour, visited post-flight to MSFC. Because of the professional relationship I had developed with NASA public affairs over the years, I was invited to meet with each crew and have them sign the tribute. Several people have told me that they hold the tribute right there with their Silver Snoopy Award.

The tribute has provided something way beyond my memories that is so incredibly tangible and will be shared for generations as a reminder of the contributions by so many. That was another check on my bucket list!

STS-133 Discovery Crew. Courtesy NASA

STS-134 Endeavour Crew (partial). Courtesy NASA

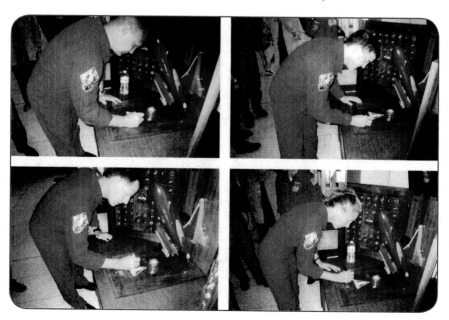

STS-135 Atlantis Crew. Courtesy NASA

April 21, 2011   **MARSHALL STAR**   8

Celebrating 30 years of space shuttle

Shuttle model created by Marshall's Scott Phillips on display in Building 4200 lobby

In commemoration of the 30th anniversary of the first flight of the space shuttle, a 1:100 scale shuttle model, created by Scott G. Phillips – a logistics engineer with Lockheed Martin Co., supporting the Marshall Space Flight Center's Engineering Directorate – is on display in the Building 4200 lobby until April 29. Two years in the making, the project is made with 20 different woods, with 18 species of wood in the orbiter alone. Pins representing every flight and plates representing each of the program's orbiters flank the model. "As a shuttle team member for over 30 years, assembling this project was bittersweet as I remembered each and every flight that the pins represent," said Phillips. "When asked where my inspiration came from, I thought about the 30-plus years that I dedicated to the program and all the people whom I came in contact with. It was not as much about the hardware but more about the dedication of those who made it happen." On April 12, 1981, people from across the world watched as space shuttle Columbia, America's first shuttle, lifted off into the Florida skies at 6 a.m. CST from Pad A of Kennedy Space Center's Launch Complex 39, beginning the STS-1 mission. Columbia returned to Earth on April 14, 1981. Marshall led the development and operation of the shuttle propulsion elements. To read more about the 30th anniversary, visit last week's Marshall Star at http://marshallstar.msfc.nasa.gov/4-14-11.pdf.

MARSHALL STAR
Vol. 51/No. 31

Marshall Space Flight Center, Alabama 35812
256-544-0030
http://www.nasa.gov/centers/marshall

The Marshall Star is published every Thursday by the Public and Employee Communications Office at the George C. Marshall Space Flight Center, National Aeronautics and Space Administration. Classified ads must be submitted no later than 4:30 p.m. Thursday to the Marshall Public and Employee Communications Office (CS20), Bldg. 4200, Room 102. Submissions should be written legibly and include the originator's name. Send e-mail submissions to: MSFC-INTERCOM@mail.nasa.gov. The Star does not publish commercial advertising of any kind.

Manager of Public and Employee Communications: Dom Amatore
Editor: Jessica Wallace Eagan

U.S. Government Printing Office 2011-723-031-00095

www.nasa.gov

PRE-SORT STANDARD
Postage & Fees PAID
NASA
Permit No. 298

Marshall Star featuring Tribute Model

In June of 2011, just weeks before the final launch of the Space Shuttle, my family and I took a short vacation to Michigan to visit Dianne's family. We returned home to 100-degree temperatures and discovered the air-conditioning unit had gone on the fritz, and Christian's favorite red belly frog had become a sad statistic. We had to endure the night in a sweltering heat that even multiple fans couldn't cool.

I arrived at work the next morning, still tired from the long drive home the day before and stressed from the heat. On my voice mail, I heard a request to attend a 9:00 meeting. I knew in my heart what it was about. I walked in to my manager's office, and he reluctantly handed me a letter. It was my turn. I was informed that my services were no longer needed on the Shuttle Program and that I would need to train a replacement who would handle my duties for the remaining weeks. My dream had been taken from me. I came so close, but I would not see to the end what I had started more than thirty years earlier. I was devastated.

After the stress of recent months, that news was the tipping point, and I blacked out. I knew the cause and I knew the solution. I would have to rely on my "gaman" to keep me focused through training my replacement and accepting my shortened end date.

For one very dark week, I worked to transition someone else to handle my remaining duties and to close the books on my Shuttle career. Then came word that there had been a miscommunication—my expertise and experience would be needed to repair cracks on the final External Tanks. I received a reprieve, and my readjusted end date was extended through the final mission. I was going to make it to the end after all!

It had been a long journey, thirty-three years in the making. Many emotions swirled through my head as I drove my family from Huntsville to Kennedy Space Center for the last Space Shuttle launch, STS-135. My thoughts took me back to 1981 when I was working twelve-hour days, seven days a week before STS-1 launched from KSC. I remembered how excited I was that

I was part of the team that launched the first vehicle. At the time, I had no idea how long the Shuttle would last. We had concerns after the Challenger and Columbia tragedies, but each time, we knew we would recover and that we would fly again. And we did. Now 135 missions later, I was about to witness the end of an era.

In keeping to my bucket-list goals, I had managed to line up a fantastic photo opportunity on the pad. The day prior to launch, I was invited to be onsite to assist in installing an infrared camera on the pad that would take pictures of the External Tank during launch. I had been the last person out of the External Tank for the first Space Shuttle flight, and now, all these years later, I would be one of the last to work with the tank for the final flight. I had been incredibly fortunate to have such a unique role in something so historic.

Scott playing his Martin guitar on the pad next to
Atlantis STS-135. Courtesy Jody Minor

We arrived a day early to make sure everything would play out smoothly. I secured my pass for the pad and everything went according to plan. While I was working on the pad and getting my photo op, my family enjoyed an afternoon at the Kennedy Space Center museum. My son Christian enjoys collecting rocks so I made sure to gather several crushed rocks from the crawler's path as a memento. I've always understood the enormity and complexity of the Space Shuttle, but standing there next to Atlantis invoked a powerful sense of what the program meant for our country. As the light filtered through the stack, it was almost like standing in front of the Statue of Liberty and realizing what that symbol means to so many people. I felt a deep sense of pride to be an American. The Shuttle, for me, had always been about the people, not the hardware. The hardware was fantastic, but it was cold and unforgiving. It was the people who enabled it to launch.

We were staying with my sister Lori in Orlando, and we had to make a decision whether to drive back to her place the night before the launch and return early the next morning or to stay local and beat the crowds that were expected. The weather was also a concern. Rain and thunderstorms were expected throughout the night. We decided to remain in Titusville, knowing the launch could be scrubbed at any moment. We monitored the launch status on our laptop throughout the night. As soon as we saw daybreak over the coast, we set out for our coveted spot onsite and waited for the countdown to begin. The weather remained unpredictable due to the possibility of strengthening cloud formations.

National Aeronautics and Space Administration

NASA

STS-135
CAR PLACARD
NASA CAUSEWAY WEST

PLACARD VALID ONLY WITH A BADGED EMPLOYEE

No more than 7 people per vehicle will be permitted at this site; NO RVs.

Government vehicles not permitted

This permit is non-transferable and may not be reproduced. Misuse of this permit may result in the removal of all occupants of this vehicle from KSC property.

EXPECT HEAVY TRAFFIC
* FRONT of Placard   Vehicle Permit No.   **1012**

STS-135 Car Placard

We met a lot of interesting people that morning and heard many amazing Shuttle stories. I had my C. F. Martin guitar and a Shuttle model in my vehicle and shared those as well. There was one particular individual who was very curious to see my art piece. I didn't recognize him at the time, but knew he looked familiar. It turned out to be astronaut Don Petit, who spent many months on the International Space Station.

The weather was "go" and then "no go" throughout the morning. We watched with excitement as it came closer and closer to the launch window, until we heard the final "go," and the countdown continued. All technical systems were held at thirty-one seconds for a camera-placement issue. My heart nearly jumped out of my chest. Surely, it wasn't the camera I helped set up that caused the countdown to stop! Thankfully, it was not. The issue was resolved, and the countdown resumed. This time, it went all the way to zero.

It was a spectacular lift off. The crowd was on their feet cheering. I took lots of pictures of my family watching with the Shuttle as a backdrop. With tears rolling down my face, I simply stood and watched in silence. It was a bittersweet moment for everyone witnessing the final launch of Atlantis on STS-135.

Lift off of Space Shuttle STS-135 on Atlantis.
Courtesy James N. Brown, Photographer

Dianne, Scott, Tyler and Christian post launch of STS-135

I was exhilarated witnessing the last launch of the Space Shuttle yet saddened knowing my own end date was nearing. When I returned to work, I felt the familiar whispers that I had witnessed with coworkers so many times over the past several years. I couldn't help chuckling to myself. It seemed absurd and rather comical to me that people think that by speaking softly in a consoling tone it would keep someone from going off the deep end. I had already decided that I wasn't going to be sad about my last day; I was going to celebrate the fact that I had the opportunity for thirty-three years and look forward to the next chapter in my life. It had been a beautiful end to my career. Through my grief, my gaman had paved a way for my creativity to take wings. The demise of the Space Shuttle Program gave flight to my passion for legacy.

At each entrance to Marshall Space Flight Center, there is a security gate. Each morning, thousands of people going to work at MSFC on Redstone Arsenal wait in line to go through these gates. You show the guards your badge, and they let you through. It is your key not only to the Center itself but also to each of the buildings within. After you wear that badge long enough, you start to feel naked without it. When employees leave their jobs at MSFC, the last thing they do is turn in their badges. Then all doors are closed to them.

This had been my workplace for most of my life, and in a very real way, it had been my life. It was surreal waking up on my last day. It was a quiet day at work, as I boxed up my belongings and removed history from my walls, including the first external tank poster given to me by the man who hired me thirty-three years earlier, I paused to reflect on the familiar surroundings, every sight and sound.

As I was removing my hard hat from the metal coat rack outside my office, I noticed a thin layer of dust had settled on it. It stopped me in my tracks. I don't recall how long I stood there, but I remember saying aloud, "Scott, your mission is complete. Take what experience the program has given you and don't fret about where you're going. Don't second-guess yourself." At that moment, I was looking forward to reinventing myself and moving forward. Somehow, the end was easier because I knew I had gone the distance.

Sometimes, we're at our best when we're going through our worst.

As I drove out Rideout Road for the last time as a Space Shuttle Team Member with the familiar MSFC Headquarters sign off to the right, I knew I wasn't leaving it behind.

I was an ordinary person with the innate desire to be extraordinary. I believe I needed to experience humble beginnings in order to recognize and appreciate a world of infinite opportunity. My unique brand of art and one-of-a-kind experiences have empowered me with long-lasting fulfillment.

I am forever connected to the lasting and mighty legacy of the Space Shuttle Program. I am honored to share the tapestry of my great adventure, the final check on my bucket list.

Thinking back of that young boy staring up at the stars with a burning desire to be part of something larger than himself and then sliding down that snow-packed hill toward the 33,000 volts, I would say that 33 electrifying years on the Space Shuttle Program was just the ticket.

The Shuttle Program now belongs to the ages, but it's not over. I am continuing the legacy of manned space flight to remind our generation of what was accomplished and to inspire and encourage future generations to keep the dream alive and what a beautiful beginning it is.

Space Shuttle Program 1981-2011

Woodism

*A person who works with their hands is a laborer.
A person who works with their hands and their
head is a craftsperson. A person who works with
their hands, their head, and their heart is an
artist. A person who works with their hands, their
head, their heart, and their soul is—was—
a Space Shuttle Team member.*

Epilogue

My longing to be a part of something larger than myself didn't end when I retired from the Shuttle Program. Weaving the tapestry of my life journey into my final bucket list item—the writing of my memoir—afforded me time for introspection and paved the road for my future.

I know and value the power of collaboration. It has enabled me to forge solid associations, including Mike Griffin, former NASA Administrator; former astronauts Brian Duffy, Eileen Collins, Mae Jemison, and Jan Davis; Robert Pearlman, founder of Collectspace, a world-class online space memorabilia community; and Dick Boak, Public Relations and Museum Curator at C. F. Martin Guitar Company. Their authenticity and high level of competence and integrity inspired me to create my own unique brand.

One of my most significant relationships was with my brother Steve. He was a major influence in shaping the person I am today, personally and professionally. In 2001, he selflessly gave one of his kidneys to his wife, Gaby. Without it, she would have died. Ten years later, that kidney failed and, with little hope for a donor, Steve learned to administer home dialysis. About the same time, he was diagnosed with lung cancer. We knew he was a fighter and we hoped for a good outcome. He fought a long and courageous battle, but succumbed to the cancer on September 11, 2013. Gaby passed away two months later. I will forever remember his legacy of unconditional love.

I am proud to have been associated with the greatest workforce of the twentieth century. With the Shuttle now part of the ages, its legacy is larger than I ever dreamed possible, and it continues to grow. The program motivated and inspired countless people around the world and opened our universe of understanding.

As people reflect on the enormity of the program and long to reconnect in a tangible way, I hope my artwork symbolizes the excellence achieved on the program, stirring others to celebrate their own memories, whether as participants or spectators. As the circle of people grows, so does the legacy.

Scott today with his world-class Space Shuttle Tribute exhibit at the Davidson Center Museum in Huntsville, AL

Woodism

Legacy is a pathway to the future.

Appendix A

Space Shuttle External Tank History

Customer: National Aeronautics and Space Administration (NASA) Marshall Space Flight Center (MSFC) Huntsville, Alabama

Contract: Design, development, test and engineering, production of the Shuttle External Tank and facilities support at NASA's Michoud Assembly Facility

Company Role: Lockheed Martin (previously Martin Marietta) manufactured the External Tank – the only major non-reusable element of the Space Shuttle – at NASA's Michoud Assembly Facility in New Orleans, LA. One tank was used for each launch.

Description: At 153.8 feet long and 27.6 feet in diameter, the External Tank was the largest element of the Space Shuttle and the structural backbone of the system. It was comprised of a forward liquid oxygen tank, aft liquid hydrogen tank and a connecting intertank. The tanks were initially made of 2219 aluminum, steel alloys, and titanium. A spray-on foam insulation material approximately one inch thick was applied to the exterior of the entire External Tank, with 282 square feet of underlying ablators, to prevent ice build-up and to protect the tank from engine and aerodynamic heating.

Post-test flight series, NASA requested Martin Marietta to trim at least 6,000 pounds from the External Tank, which weighed 76,000 pounds. New fabricating techniques, material and design changes yielded a 10,000 pound weight savings and resulted in the first Lightweight Tank weighing 66,000 pounds. This translated to an almost equal payload increase for the shuttle. The seventh tank and all succeeding tanks through ET-94 were of the Lightweight configuration.

Lockheed Martin (formerly Martin Marietta) then began building the next generation of the External Tank, the Super Lightweight Tank, which weighed 58,500 pounds. Featuring design changes and an aluminum-lithium alloy and weighing some 7,500 pounds less than the Lightweight Tank, the Super Lightweight Tanks were vital for building and supplying the International Space Station. The first Super Lightweight Tank, ET-96, lifted off June 2, 1998, powering Shuttle Mission STS-91.

*Tank Capacity:	Total:	535,277 gallons
		740,159 kg
		1,610,000 lbs.
	Liquid Oxygen:	145,138 gallons
		625,850 kg
		1,380,000 lbs.
	Liquid Hydrogen:	390,139 gallons
		104,308 kg
		230,000 lbs.

*Approximate

Tank Size:	Length:	153.8 feet	4,688.0 cm
	Diameter:	27.6 feet	840.0 cm
	Hydrogen Tank Length:	96.7 feet	2,947.0 cm
	Oxygen Tank Length:	54.6 feet	1,664.0 cm
	Intertank Length:	22.5 feet	686.0 cm
	Lightweight Tank Weight:	66,000 lbs. empty	29,932 kg
		1,676,000 lbs. loaded	760,091 kg
	Super Lightweight Tank:	58,500 lbs. empty	26,536 kg
		1,668,500 lbs. loaded	756,832 kg

| **Propellant** | *Liquid Oxygen: | 159,480 lbs./min. or 16,800 gal/min. |
| **Flow:** | *Liquid Hydrogen: | 29,640 lbs./min. or 45,283 gal/min. |

*Note:	Liquid Oxygen Weight	=	71.1 lbs./cu. ft.
	Liquid Hydrogen Weight	=	4.4 lbs./cu. ft.
	Liquid Oxygen Temp	=	-297 degrees F
	Liquid Hydrogen Temp	=	-423 degrees F

Nominal	Altitude:	69 statute miles
Separation:		60 nautical miles
		111 kilometers
	Downrange:	805 statute miles
		700 nautical miles
		1,297 kilometers

Operation: The External Tank supplied liquid propellants to the Orbiter through a 17-inch diameter feed line and absorbed tremendous thrust loads produced at launch by the Orbiter's three main engines and by the Solid Rocket Boosters. The tank emptied in about 8-1/2 minutes and then separated from the

Orbiter. Almost the entire tank burned up during re-entry. Any debris that did not burn up fell into a predetermined area of the Pacific or Indian Ocean.

Past

Performance: NASA launched the Space Shuttle 135 times.

Launch Dates:

STS-1	4/12/81	ET-1	STS-71	6/27/95	ET-70
STS-2	11/12/81	ET-2	STS-70	7/13/95	ET-71
STS-3	3/22/82	ET-3	STS-69	9/7/95	ET-72
STS-4	6/27/82	ET-4	STS-73	10/20/95	ET-73
STS-5	11/11/82	ET-5	STS-74	11/12/95	ET-74
STS-6	4/4/83	ET-8	STS-72	1/11/96	ET-75
STS-7	6/18/83	ET-6	STS-75	2/22/96	ET-76
STS-8	8/30/83	ET-9	STS-76	3/22/96	ET-77
STS-9	11/28/83	ET-11	STS-77	5/19/96	ET-78
STS 41-B	2/3/84	ET-10	STS-78	6/20/96	ET-79
STS 41-C	4/6/84	ET-12	STS-79	9/16/96	ET-82
STS 41-D	8/30/84	ET-13	STS-80	11/19/96	ET-80
STS 41-G	10/5/84	ET-15	STS-81	1/12/97	ET-83
STS 51-A	11/8/85	ET-16	STS-82	2/11/97	ET-81
STS 51-C	1/24/85	ET-14	STS-83	4/4/97	ET-84
STS 51-D	4/12/85	ET-18	STS-84	5/15/97	ET-85
STS 51-B	4/29/85	ET-17	STS-94	7/1/97	ET-86
STS 51-G	6/17/85	ET-20	STS-85	8/7/97	ET-87
STS 51-F	7/29/85	ET-19	STS-86	9/26/97	ET-88
STS 51-I	8/27/85	ET-21	STS-87	11/19/97	ET-89
STS 51-J	10/3/85	ET-25	STS-89	1/23/98	ET-90
STS 61-A	10/30/85	ET-24	STS-90	4/17/98	ET-91
STS 61-B	11/26/85	ET-22	STS-91	6/2/98	ET-96
STS 61-C	1/12/86	ET-30	STS-95	10/29/98	ET-98
STS 51-L	1/28/86	ET-26	STS-88	12/4/98	ET-97
STS-26	9/29/88	ET-28	STS-96	5/27/99	ET-100
STS-27	12/2/88	ET-23	STS-93	7/23/99	ET-99
STS-29	3/13/89	ET-36	STS-103	12/20/99	ET-101
STS-30	5/4/89	ET-29	STS-99	2/11/00	ET-92

STS-28	8/8/89	ET-31	STS-101	5/19/00	ET-102
STS-34	10/18/89	ET-27	STS-106	9/8/00	ET-103
STS-33	11/22/89	ET-38	STS-92	10/11/00	ET-104
STS-32	1/9/90	ET-32	STS-97	12/1/00	ET-105
STS-36	2/28/90	ET-33	STS-98	2/7/01	ET-106
STS-31	4/24/90	ET-34	STS-102	3/8/01	ET-107
STS-41	10/6/90	ET-39	STS-100	4/19/01	ET-108
STS-38	11/15/90	ET-40	STS-104	7/12/01	ET-109
STS-35	12/2/90	ET-35	STS-105	8/10/01	ET-110
STS-37	4/5/91	ET-37	STS-108	12/5/01	ET-111
STS-39	4/28/91	ET-46	STS-109	3/1/02	ET-112
STS-40	6/5/91	ET-41	STS-110	4/8/02	ET-114
STS-43	8/2/91	ET-47	STS-111	6/5/02	ET-113
STS-48	9/12/91	ET-42	STS-112	10/7/02	ET-115
STS-44	11/24/91	ET-53	STS-113	11/23/02	ET-116
STS-42	1/22/92	ET-52	STS-107	1/16/03	ET-93
STS-45	3/24/92	ET-44	STS-114	7/26/05	ET-121
STS-49	5/7/92	ET-43	STS-121	7/4/06	ET-119
STS-50	6/25/92	ET-50	STS-115	9/9/06	ET-118
STS-46	7/31/92	ET-48	STS-116	12/10/06	ET-123
STS-47	9/12/92	ET-45	STS-117	6/8/07	ET-124
STS-52	10/22/92	ET-55	STS-118	8/8/07	ET-117
STS-53	12/2/92	ET-49	STS-120	10/23/07	ET-120
STS-54	1/13/93	ET-51	STS-122	2/7/08	ET-125
STS-56	4/8/93	ET-54	STS-123	3/11/08	ET-128
STS-55	4/26/93	ET-56	STS-124	5/31/08	ET-128
STS-57	6/21/93	ET-58	STS-126	11/15/08	ET-129
STS-51	9/12/93	ET-59	STS-119	3/15/09	ET-127
STS-58	10/18/93	ET-57	STS-125	5/11/09	ET-130
STS-61	12/2/93	ET-60	STS-127	7/15/09	ET-131
STS-60	2/3/94	ET-61	STS-128	8/28/09	ET-132
STS-62	3/4/94	ET-62	STS-129	11/16/09	ET-133
STS-59	4/9/94	ET-63	STS-130	2/8/10	ET-134
STS-65	7/8/94	ET-64	STS-131	4/5/10	ET-135
STS-64	9/9/94	ET-66	STS-132	5/14/10	ET-136
STS-68	9/30/94	ET-65	STS-133	2/24/11	ET-137
STS-66	11/3/94	ET-67	STS-134	5/16/11	ET-122
STS-63	2/3/95	ET-68	STS-135	7/8/11	ET-138
STS-67	3/2/95	ET-69			

Tank Surplus:

ET-7	Never built (transitioned to the Lightweight Tank (LWT) Program)
ET-94/LWT	Never flown (dissected for CAIB Report post-Columbia disaster)
ET-95	Never built (transitioned to Super Lightweight Tank Program)
ET-139	Never built (subassemblies only)
ET-140	Never built (subassemblies only)
ET-141	Never built (subassemblies only)

Test Tanks:

MPTA	Located at Alabama Space and Rocket Center in Huntsville, Alabama
GVTA	Scrapped out (parts only)
STA	Currently located at Wings of Dreams Aviation Museum in Starke, Florida

Milestones: Martin Marietta delivered the first External Tank (MPTA) for tests to NASA on September 7, 1977. Michoud delivered the first flight ready tank (ET-1) to NASA on June 29, 1979.

The first unpainted tank (saving approximately 600 lbs.) launched as part of the STS-3 mission on March 22, 1982. The first Lightweight Tank propelled the STS-6 mission on April 4, 1983. The final Heavyweight Tank launched with STS-7 on June 18, 1983. The first Super Lightweight Tank launched STS-91 on June 2, 1998.

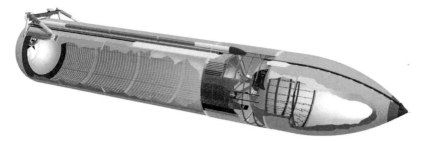

External tank partial cutaway

Manned Space Flight Poster—135 Flights

Appendix B

Space the Eternal©

Original poem by Ralph E. Young, NASA 1991

Truly the final frontier...or is it to be an ending...?
Space – To man a quest, an intellectual test of numbers, hardware, habitat, and hopefully..., his own existence for our tomorrows. It is hoped space is a future to nurture and embellish collective accomplishments, never to relive past tragedies, but only to increase our learning and deserved respect. It is its ever progressing blackness punctuated by moments of awe inspiring light that will enable the human creature to be drawn to it liken unto a siren, so that someday he may be allowed to gaze upon this solid earth as a point of light, from which his own terrestrial inhabitant ancestors sprang. Who knows the light we seek, may be in future millennia's quest out our light with the same thirst for the "What's out there?" we so often cast at the heavens. Lest we do not forget, as we would approach a fawn – not too soon, not too fast, not with weapons, but with the inquisitiveness and wide eyed wonder of a man child.. We must expurgate the appetite for

conquest, or for dreadnaught machines to pillage and maim all in the name of exploration. For if we do not, it will escape our grasp. We will never again see its beauty, but evoke a summons to audit from its archives, caused by our own marauding obtrusiveness. If not kept in check, we could suffer its wrath, be entombed in its darkness, or annihilated by its very nature.

Space...don't break it.
Space the Eternal©
Editor's Choice Award
Poetry.com
2006
(Reprinted with permission)

Acknowledgments

I would like to thank everyone who helped make this book possible:

My loving wife, Dianne: without her patience to listen to all my stories, her creative writing skills, and ability to capture my voice, this book would still be rattling around in my head.

My children, Christian and Tyler, for their unconditional love and for allowing us the time to write this book.

My parents, Dick and Mary Lue Phillips, for my life and for their courage to take risks.

My siblings, Debbie, Steve, Lori, and Susan for the childhood lessons they taught me and for their continued support and encouragement.

My in-laws, Ty and Lois Cobb, Gail Shanaver, and Cheryl Webb and their families.

My brother-in-law, Rob Berkley, life coach extraordinaire.

Editor, Kacy Cook, words cannot express our gratitude for her professional advice and assistance in editing and polishing this manuscript.

Fellow space enthusiast, Gary Milgrom, for his support and skill in designing the book cover and photo enhancements.

Longtime friend, David Little, for his unconditional support, collaboration, and encouragement.

Lifeline Children's Services, for believing in us; our lives are enriched beyond words.

Former NASA Administrator, Dr. Michael Griffin, for his wisdom and support.

Former NASA employee, Craig Sumner, for his encouragement during my career and collaboration on the ET-70 story.

Lockheed Martin technical writer, Mark "Woketman" Pokrywka, for sharing his expertise.

Author, David Hitt (*Bold They Rise, Home in the Sky: Skylab,* and *Homesteading Space)* for his collaboration on historical accuracy.

Friends and colleagues who took the time to read the manuscript with the promise of providing unbiased feedback, including NASA employee and author of the poem, *Space the Eternal,* Ralph Young; NASA Goddard Space Center employee, Mark Hubbard; John and Peggy Cranston, Sara Howard, and Brad Bradford.

Dr. Richard Tate, Founder of Tate Publishing, and his professional staff for catching our vision.

Facebook family and Collectspace community for their support and desire to keep the legacy alive.

The dedicated men and women on the Space Shuttle Program who caught my vision.

The courageous astronauts who risked (and the 14 who gave) their lives for the pursuit of knowledge and human understanding.

Contact/Media

Connect with Scott for more information, speaking opportunities, or to display his world-class Space Shuttle Exhibit:

E-mail: scottphillips.wood@gmail.com
Web site: www.removebeforeflightbook.com
Facebook: https://www.facebook.com/scottphillips.wood
Facebook (Pecan Dynasty): https://www.facebook.com/Pecan Dynasty
Twitter: https://twitter.com: Shuttleman01

Articles

http://www.woodworkersjournal.com/Ezine/Articles/Scott-Phillips-
    Launched-Into-Space-Shuttle-Models-8572.aspx
http://www.collectspace.com/ubb/Forum16/HTML/000683.html
http://www.collectspace.com/ubb/Forum3/HTML/004305.html
http://www.collectspace.com/ubb/Forum9/HTML/001869.html
http://www.collectspace.com/ubb/Forum38/HTML/001403.html
http://www.collectspace.com/ubb/Forum41/HTML/000356.html
http://www.collectspace.com/ubb/Forum16/HTML/000067.html
http://marshallstar.msfc.nasa.gov/12-7-00.pdf

http://marshallstar.msfc.nasa.gov/4-21-11.pdf

Media Clips

https://www.facebook.com/photo.php?v=10151574025839171&set=v
b.501289170&type=2&theater

http://whnt.com/2012/07/06/local-artist-preserving-the-shuttle-
program-in-his-own-way/

http://www.martinguitar.com/images/downloads/newsletter/Vol_31.pdf

Recommended Links

Collectspace: http://www.collectspace.com/

Martin Guitar Company: http://www.martinguitar.com/

Marshall Space Flight Center Homepage: http://www.nasa.gov/centers/
marshall/home/

Kennedy Space Center Homepage: http://www.nasa.gov/centers/ken
nedy/home/

Michoud Facility Homepage: http://www.nasa.gov/centers/marshall/
michoud/

Stennis Space Center Homepage: http://www.nasa.gov/centers/sten
nis/home/

Space and Rocket Center Homepage: http://www.rocketcenter.com/